© Copyright 2013

Elizabeth Richardson AUSTRALIA

Print Edition

ISBN 978-0-9872612-0-5

The intent of this author is to share information of a general nature that may assist others to feel better. In the event you use any of the information in this book for yourself, which is your constitutional right, the author and the publisher assume no responsibility for your actions. You are responsible for you.

This book is licensed for your personal enjoyment. We always appreciate being acknowledged when you repost, reprint, or reuse any part of the material contained herein.

Thank you for respecting the integrity of this work.

Find out more about the author at
https://elizabethrichardson.info

Find out more about the book at
https://confessions.elizabethrichardson.info

Join in the conversation at:
https://facebook.com/500confessions

Preface

500 Confessions has been likened to a modern-day "Course In Miracles" with a soothing, thought provoking and a sometimes funny twist.

It doesn't preach or instruct, it isn't intended to teach or even guide, but it will take you on an adventure into your own life, provide an open-hearted look at relationships, reveal your existing beliefs and attitudes and help you automatically choose more life-enhancing ones.

It's been written in a unique way that tends to comfort doubts, relax fears, inspire hope and a give you a good laugh all rolled into one.

It does contain some swearing, talks about sex and has a small amount of other adult only material … but it's just like life seen as it really is and how you too, might make it even better.

The intended audience is readers aged 25+ who want a practical, warm and fun way to be entertained, to be able to hear their own inner guidance more clearly, to open their hearts and expand their mind.

The book particularly appeals to those who resonate with the teachings of Abraham Hicks™ or Conversations With God by Neale Donald Walsch, yet attracts people of all beliefs, lifestyles and faiths, atheists and Christians alike.

How This Book Came to Be

Out of the Worst Relationship, Came the Most Amazing Gifts

Not so long ago, a relationship which was incredibly loving, spontaneous, and fun suddenly changed into something quite different. I found myself writing to find comfort, clarity and stability.

Born from the turmoil were insights, each received easily, quickly and effortlessly as I received answers to other people's questions as well as my own.

Early on I could see in my mind the cover of a best-selling book, I was given the format, the words kept being drawn through me, the writing was inspired and people were asking for more. One man requested to be able to purchase the writings in print, digitally and audibly and even specified where he wanted to be able to purchase them from.

There were SO MANY requests that, from its conception, the writings had already taken on a life of their own.

It was created because I needed it ... and YOU asked for it. So I will step aside and let the words speak for themselves, let the message be what resonates, let the writings be what encourages others to find their own insight and let the confessions be the catalyst for alignment – not the author!

From the words of CONFESSION #212 … I DON'T NEED YOU TO LOVE ME … as much as you are loving who you are becoming. I don't require others to follow, I'd rather they follow their heart, their dreams, their passion. I don't need fans, I prefer that you fan the flames of desire now burning inside and I don't want to be worshiped, I encourage you to stand in awe of your precious uniqueness & align in wholeness with your own blessed soul.

Special Acknowledgements

With humble thanks for all the problems that cried out for solutions, for all the questions that begged for answers and for all the profound insights that were (and still are) inspired from a greater source than one person alone could ever produce, and ESPECIALLY stimulated by the teachings of Abraham-Hicks™

With deepest appreciation to my own soul, higher self, GOD, universal energy, my inner being and infinite intelligence for inspiring the words, expanding the wisdom, spouting forth profound answers, providing eternal solutions and brightly guiding my path.

And I appreciate YOU for being here, for wanting more, for seeking clarity, for being open to receiving YOUR answers, for giving me the occasional confrontations and for being such an integral part of the incredible expansion that this experience has given me.

I have EVERYONE to thank; especially the readers who have already called forth into being, this BOOK OF CONFESSIONS to rock your world, inspire your mind, uplift your spirits & soothe your soul. ~ Elizabeth Richardson

What Other People Are Saying ...

Since the conception of "500 Confessions" directly on the pages of Facebook, it's received thousands of comments, requests and testimonials. Here's just a snippet of what other people are saying.

You are an angel planting wisdom in the humans' heart ... Thanks! – Yármila Durand

I've just finished studying your confessions and they are instilling hope, expectation, faith, optimism and above all an attitude of 'Feeling Good' in all situations of life. They are my constant companion. They mold us to love our self. – Shaukat Charania

You articulate what it is to live a peaceful existence within ourselves here. Very profound! – Ley-Ann Clarke

Every time I read your words, I grow spiritually ... it is as if I take that one word or two and slowly I let them sink in ... thanks for your sharing you intimate self with us ... – Patrizia Rampone

These words are like a prayer. Their effect is invigorating. – Ravie Kathuria

You so eloquently capture through written word, my very thoughts and feelings. Thank you for the work you do. – Lucy Bordonaro

I really enjoy reading your confessions! Sometimes they are just what I need to find insight. – Shawn Maskel

This is indeed a Life prayer. Thanks Elizabeth! Your words are a blessing. – Sunitha Choudhry

I am here to thank you for all the wonderful things you write and with all those words you have helped me grow mentally to a better level ... a level where I could not imagine myself sometimes ago ... I am happy with who I am. – Hina V Chaudhary

Your confessions always bring me into the vortex ... I just love them so much, and I love you so much. Keep confessing ... I just like the feelings of 'high' they provide me. – Zetty Zakaria

Wow. You put Abraham in understandable English! What a blessing! – Joni Blumstein

Amazing again ER! I sometimes feel you are writing what I have been thinking and feeling. – Laurie Kendzulak

You give reality to my emotions and inner knowing ... over and over and over again. – Alethea Lobo

Tasty treats to align one's soul to today's true beat ... one woman's wisdom echoing millions of hearts. – Lara Ackroyd

If this isn't an answer to my prayer this morning! Thank you. CONFESSION #281, I've already put on my desktop. – Judy Morgan

They help us move forward with a positive frame of mind ... they multiply joy and subtract worries. – Raushni Srivastava

*I always look forward to reading your words. They make me a better person! Thank you so much. – Jo-anne Mmela
Best Advice I've ever received! Thanks Elizabeth! – Di Davis*

These are profound. Thank you for offering them. – Mary Jones

You make such a difference in this world! – Patrick Carney

ER I read your valuable confessions daily and they are nutritious food for my soul. – Raushni Srivastava

Your writings have been inspiring and helped me through some tough times. Thank you. – Jaclyn Bain

I always look forward to reading your confessions during the day. They have helped me to keep positive, strong and to stay true to myself. – Michelle Niese Hinshaw Steen

These Confessions have been a great inspirational source for me. – Sutra Dewi Haruni

Wonderful … so simple … really … no long-complicated rules or steps … just easy to understand concepts … glorious! – Shanti Zimmermann

You are Poetry in Motion! I Love the freedom and Power you bring to others just by being you! – Carolee Dalton (Happiness Coach)

Your words have been an incredible catalyst in my life for peace and well-being. The confessions are so lighthearted, like a breath of fresh air. - Kristian Hodko

The world needs your confessions. – Dimple Pandey

500 CONFESSIONS

(Book 1)

to rock your world, inspire your mind, uplift your spirits

&

soothe your soul.

CONFESSION # 1 ...

Sometimes I find great pleasure in BEING annoyingly happy.

CONFESSION # 2 ...

I'M FULL OF MYSELF

... and when I am full of ME, I am overflowing with love for others. It cannot help but pour out of me. The pressure must be released and then I become like my own essence, eternally flowing love through the depths of my soul.

CONFESSION # 3 ...

I TELL LOTS OF LIES

... and then live like they are already true.

For months I imagined how I would feel if I were in a relationship. I had conversations about the wonderful things a relationship brings to my life. I wrote on Facebook as if I was deeply in love to the point that when I announced I had started a relationship, most people thought that I was already in one.

I LIVE MY DREAMS INTO LIFE

I imagine I have something before it even shows up. I pretend I am someone before anyone else even notices. I behave as if the world is my oyster ... and then as if by magic, it opens up and presents me with the clearest and shiniest pearl in the whole wide world.

BUT WHAT ABOUT TELLING THE TRUTH?

Everyone tells lies and the worst sort are when we tell ourselves we aren't good enough, rich enough, smart enough, attractive enough, thin enough or worthy enough ... because whether it's considered truth or lie, what we keep on telling ourselves, becomes our reality.

CONFESSION # 4 ...

I DON'T HAVE ANY PATIENCE

I just hand everything I can't control over to the "universe" to manage for me ... then go out and find as many things to laugh about, to enjoy, to have fun with and to appreciate as I possibly can! That's when things fall perfectly into place.

CONFESSION # 5 ...

I LOVE SEX

... I love porn, I love orgasm and I love my body.

I have absolutely NO RULES about what's appropriate for me or anyone else. If something feels good, I do it again, and again, and again. I myself decide what's right for me,

... not the church, not my parents, not my family, not society and not even my mate.

CONFESSION # 6 ...

I'M NOT IN LOVE WITH MY MATE

I'm in love with me, and when I'm in love with me the person closest to me is showered mightily with affection, praise, love and appreciation.

I ONLY see the best in him, I ONLY talk about his finer points, I believe in him more than he believes in himself and when I flow love to this degree, both of us can do nothing else but thrive.

(For further thoughts about what love really is, see CONFESSION #129 ... I LOVE MANY THINGS)

CONFESSION # 7 ...

I DON'T GIVE A SH*T WHAT YOU THINK OF ME

It's not my job to conform to your standards so you can feel secure, so you can find peace, so you can be happy. It is each individual's task to find comfort, stillness and joy in the essence of their own soul.

Each time we ask someone to be different to who they really are, we drag them away from expressing their own desires, living their truth, following their calling and forging the most important life of all ... their own!

CONFESSION # 8 ...

I DON'T FACE REALITY

... but I do notice it and decide how I'd like it to be instead.

Then I imagine that, think about that, talk about that, write about that, believe that, know that and then pretty soon, watch as a brand new reality unfolds in front of me.

Reality is for people who have no idea they can turn towards what they'd prefer to experience and attract/create something so much better instead.

(Imagine if you were a racing car driver or horse rider, would it be best to look at the collision course your vehicle is taking you on, or towards where you REALLY want to go!)

CONFESSION # 9 ...

I HAVE MY OWN GOD

It never made sense to me that God would judge someone in the same way that humans do, that he'd feel so powerless to demand that we should worship him, that he'd declare that one church was better than another, that the very act of love that brought each of us into the world would be "made wrong" in certain circumstances OR that we must be different sexes to even have a relationship.

Instead of choosing the same God I was taught to believe in, I've developed a powerfully intimate, ongoing relationship with the God I know, who is totally loving and accepting of all of us.

CONFESSION # 10 ...

I HAVE AN ADDICTION

… to feeling fabulous, having fun, laughing lots, making love, uplifting others, enjoying the sun, getting inspired, being happy, remembering good times, having beautiful things, enjoying the magnificence of nature, sharing life with someone special, doing what I want, when I want, with whoever I want, as often as I want … and watching as it positively effects those around me.

CONFESSION # 11 ...

I KNOW HOW TO GIVE UP AN ADDICTION

Decide what I want to be addicted to instead!

I can get addicted to love, life, to happiness, to bliss – I get to choose! Then ... I NEVER need to talk about my past again. I NEVER need to evaluate why I got there or how I got there and I NEVER EVER need to prove to anyone else that I've changed.

Just BE who I want to be and move quietly and gently towards the future of my dreams.

CONFESSION # 12 ...

I LOVE GOSSIP

... but gossip in a way that lifts people up, not puts them down, gossip in a way that makes people shine, not dulls their existence, gossip in a way that makes others feel good and enhances their experience of life, and hey, I think you're amazing and I'm gonna tell other people too, mostly when you can't hear ... so there!

CONFESSION # 13 ...

I DON'T THINK MONOGAMY IS RIGHT OR WRONG

... but I do know that each person should honour what feels right for them.

No matter what society thinks, no matter what our parents said, no matter what we were taught by our religions, if we line up our thoughts, our beliefs and live true to our own desire, we will attract other people who believe the same things ... and can also allow those who don't, to peacefully follow their chosen path too.

CONFESSION # 14 ...

SOMETIMES I DELIGHT IN STARTING RIOTS ... lol

 ... by pushing peoples buttons, by making them think, by stretching the boundaries of what's commonly acceptable, by speaking about topics that are taboo, by sharing a different point of view, by opening my mind from the depths of my heart ... RELAX ... all is well ... there is method in my madness!

CONFESSION # 15 ...

I DON'T MAKE PROMISES

A promise is a pledge we make in an "attempt" to repair a mistake we made in the past, to keep what we have in the present the same way forever, or to make the future more predictable. Promises we make to other people just to keep them happy are unsustainable, unwise and generally untruthful. The best promise I can ever make is that I will do my best to remain true to myself.

CONFESSION # 16 …

I WON'T BE GOING TO HEAVEN WHEN I DIE

… I'm already there!

Heaven isn't a place - it's a "state of being" which I feel inside when I allow the goodness of life to flow through me. It isn't something I need to prove my worthiness in order to achieve or fight to gain admission. It is most easily experienced when I relax, quieten my mind and feel that deep sense of peace, stillness and oneness inside my own heart.

CONFESSION # 17 ...

SANTA IS NO BETTER THAN SATAN

Religions created Satan in an attempt to manipulate others into behaving in a certain way so they can receive good stuff when they die.

Parents created Santa in an attempt to manipulate children into behaving in a certain way so they can receive good stuff while they're alive.

I won't apologize for bursting your bubble; we use stupid stuff to try and control people all the time.

CONFESSION # 18 ...

I OFTEN DO THINGS THAT OTHERS WOULD DISAPPROVE OF

... but I don't make a big thing out of it, I don't make someone else wrong because of it, I don't try to get other people to agree with me before I do it, I don't get involved in conversations about it and I don't FIGHT to get it.

Fighting for my rights keep the very things I don't want active inside me.

Integrity (living in the way that's right for me) is an inner journey, and one I choose to take quietly, gently and privately, as often as I can.

CONFESSION # 19 ...

MASTURBATING IS GOOD FOR ME

People who are having regular orgasms rarely complain about anything ... LOL ... I've had as many spiritual connections during orgasm than during meditation. It is generally one experience in life that makes people feel good, unless guilt from religious teachings has tainted the experience.

CONFESSION # 20 …

MY LIFE IS OUT OF CONTROL

… so I've handed the finer details over to a higher power to manage for me … and I know without a shadow of a doubt that no matter what my bank account says, no matter what state the economy is in, no matter what drama is going on in the world, no matter how my mate is behaving, my real job is to find as many things as possible to love and appreciate about what I've already been given.

CONFESSION # 21 ...

SOMETIMES I'M BAD ... but,

I was born to be happy, not to behave.
I was born to follow my dreams, not to chase the visions of others.
I was born to love with all of my heart, not to be afraid that my heart might break.
I was born to enjoy this moment, to feel its passion, to play, to laugh and to follow my inspiration.
I was born to live fully, to love unconditionally, to grow gracefully, to contribute quietly, to laugh heartily, to build people up.
I was born to live in harmony with my higher self and all of life.

I was born to be free, and I was born to be ME!

CONFESSION # 22 ...

I THINK NUMEROLOGY IS CRAP

… but my friends on Facebook now number 2222 … cool! I'm also a double master number 22 … powerful! And I find pleasure in claiming anything that feels good as the start of something even more wonderful, even more spectacular, even more intoxicating and expect it to expand my mind and open my heart wider than before. And what I declare, what I expect, what I intend, is what I become.

Was it a fluke, or was it the universe conspiring to make this something really special? It is also CONFESSION # 22. My favourite number in the world and the day of my birth January 22.

CONFESSION # 23 ...

I LOOK FORWARD TO DYING

… to return to where I came from, to go happily and healthfully when my time is done.

I decided that death is a blessing instead of a curse.
I believe good things will happen instead of expecting the worst.
I imagine the peace and let go of the strife,
I focus on what's wonderful and have a great life.

CONFESSION # 24 ...

I APPROVE OF DRUGS

What each person chooses as their way to get relief from mental, emotional or physical pain is no better or worse than my need to seek peace amidst turmoil or find food when I am hungry.

When I listen to my own inner guidance, I know what feels right for me. Minding my own business, tending to my own alignment and living as an example of what I believe, is the best way to empower others to do the same.

CONFESSION # 25 ...

I AM COMPLETELY SELFISH

I consider myself and my relationship with my own "inner contentment" to be the most important of all. When I am aligned, when I am in love with life, when I am being who I want to be, I have the most value to give to my friends, to my enemies, to my loved ones and to the world.

CONFESSION # 26 …

I DON'T CARE ABOUT YOU

… It's YOUR job to care about you.

In the moment I step in to care more for you than what you do for yourself, I take away YOUR power and give away my own. The best I can do is live as an example of what I believe … and by the clarity of my example, by shining the light, by illuminating the path, I set both of us free to be who we came to be … powerful, loving, intentional creators.

CARING IS TAUGHT BEHAVIOR … it usually started when our parents decided we should care more about what they wanted than for what we knew was right for us at the time. We were encouraged to move further away from our centre, our source, our knowing, our nature … simply because they had felt disconnected from their own … Then we spend the rest of our lives trying to recover it!

When we do recover our natural nature … we end up being more authentic, more charismatic, more magnetic, more admired, more trusted, more thoughtful and the greatest role model of all … one who lives in complete integrity with their own truth.

CONFESSION # 27 ...

I LOVE EVERYONE

There is not one person in my life I don't get great value from, and the ones that often give me more than most are those who are completely different to me, those who disagree with me, those who challenge me, those who have different beliefs than me ... They provide the greatest reason to grow, to expand my mind, to open my heart wider and be more of who I am ... unconditionally loving at my core.

CONFESSION # 28 …

I DON'T MISS OTHERS WHEN THEY'RE GONE

Instead I can imagine how it felt to be with them and then bask in the memory, as if it's happening right now.

I never need to feel loss, when I stay connected to my own sense of self, when I keep reaching for relief inside from whatever is making me feel unsettled on the outside, when I keep imaging the best possible outcome for the future, no matter what had come into my experience in the past.

Loss is only something I notice when I forget the incredible person I know I am, I dismiss the amazing person I know you are and I ignore the magnificent power of life to bring me everything I've asked for in perfect universal timing and in the most magical ways possible.

The only thing I ever need is my connection to love, my closeness to God, the union with my own soul. When I feel that again, I remember just how much I am an integral part of everything that was, everything that is now and everything that ever will be.

CONFESSION # 29 ...

FEELING GOOD IS THE MOST IMPORTANT THING TO ME

... then I'm connected more powerfully to my own inner guidance.

I write clearer, I hear better and I'm naturally inspired as to what to do next - every time! If thinking about something ceases to feel good, then I think about, talk about and do something else that does.

There are a plethora of things to choose from and anything at all will do.

IF IT FEELS GOOD ... I do it.
IF IT MAKES ME SMILE ... I think about it.
IF IT BRIGHTENS MY EMOTIONS ... I remember it.
IF IT MAKES MY HEART SING ... I talk about it.
IF IT SOUNDS LIKE GOOD NEWS ... I share it.
IF IT MOVES ME TOWARDS THE LIFE I DREAM OF LIVING ... I indulge in it completely.

CONFESSION # 30 …

I PRACTICE FEELING GOOD

As I train myself to focus on things that feel better each day … when something does happen that upsets my applecart, I bounce back really quickly.

I don't cry over the spilled fruit,
I don't go on a "search and destroy mission" to find out who did it and why,
I don't publish a "what to do when your boyfriend doesn't like your melons" Facebook page.
I don't give it a second thought at all.

I just make juice out of the bruised fruit, find an exciting new place to park my cart or go off to play in the orchard instead.

CONFESSION # 31 ...

I LOVE HAVING A MAN TAKE CHARGE

... to have his way with me, to make me melt into a pile of giggling girlishness,

... to turn on my heart, to relax me, to plan, to protect, to provide,

... to turn on my mind by saying how he will touch me, fondle me, kiss me, make love to me,

... to turn on my body, to gaze at me, to admire me, to expose me, to dominate me, to take me lovingly and open me in a way I have never been opened before. Aaaaaaaaaaahhhh!

He treats everything he owns with pride, care, love and attention, and when I trust him completely without question or doubt, always proves to me that I'm right. My positive belief and reinforcement brings it into being.

CONFESSION # 32 ...

I DON'T ASK OTHER PEOPLE FOR ADVICE

… the best source of all comes from inside me.

It's easiest to hear my own inner knowing, when I put myself in an expanded vibrational state by meditating, walking in nature, using incantations, dancing like a lunatic, getting happy or whatever makes me feel high and then I allow infinite intelligence to bring me what I need. And when I am ready to receive, the message is clearly given - every time!

CONFESSION # 33 ...

IT'S IMPOSSIBLE TO OFFEND ME

… I take EVERYTHING as a compliment!

Your attention to my perceived defects, faults, dysfunctions, failings and flaws says more about you than it does about me. Your attention to my magnificence says that you see clearly your own reflection shining brightly within you. And I know who you really are inside … a powerful, majestic, amazing giver of unconditional love.

CONFESSION # 34 ...

I HAVE AN AMAZING LIFE

... not because I was given some special gift, not because I have everything I could possible need, not because I was born lucky and not because of good karma. I choose how I want to experience life each day, with as much peace, bliss, joy, elation and ecstasy as I can possibly allow ... and with a little bit of drama thrown in just for fun ;-)

CONFESSION # 35 …

I CAN'T HELP YOU

… there's NOTHING wrong with you.

Your attention to your own perceived problems and the failing of others to help you in the way you think they should, keeps you stuck right where you are. Therapy is a way humans use to exchange money by first deciding someone else actually has a problem and then pretending they can fix it.

Only YOU can change your focus and give full attention to what you desire to create instead.

CONFESSION # 36 ...

I AM A "USER"

I USE MY MATE ... as an outlet to flow love, as a reason to open my heart and expand my mind. I use him for sex, the beautiful things he provides, company during the day, fabulous dinners at night, to appreciate his thoughtful gifts and help define what I desire to create in the future. I use him to provide for me in ways that encourage growth and contribution ... and that make him feel proud.

I USE FACEBOOK ... as a place to have fun, as a platform to meet others, as a way to share my thoughts, as a distraction from stress, as a method to practice my writing and as a source of brilliant entertainment.

I USE YOU ... to provide inspiration, to broaden my skills, to enhance my fulfilment, to draw answers through me, to give me the best reason to be here and explore my own purpose for living.

I USE GOD ... to guide me (through my emotions), to give me wisdom (through my mind), to live through me (through my physical body), to inspire me (through my soul) and to help me contribute profoundly to the expansion of the entire universe.

CONFESSION # 37 ...

I HAVE NO SYMPATHY FOR ANYONE

Feeling bad does NOT help anyone else feel better.

I don't pretend to understand their dilemma; instead I form part of the solution. I keep my spirits raised and uplift them, maintain my loving state and soothe them, imagine how they really want to feel and call them gently towards it. When I'm in a heightened state, my thoughts are naturally uplifting, my words are inspired and my actions are guided by a force far greater than you or I can fathom.

HOW DO I SOOTHE THEM? ... With words of encouragement "this too will pass", with a story of hope "remember how it all worked out last time", with a belief that "there is a blessing hidden in all adversity", with a knowing that "they will bounce back even better than before".

CONFESSION # 38 ...

I FIND IT EASY TO GET OVER AN EX

If I justify the ending of a relationship by focusing on the bad things that happened, I have moved SO far from the present moment that I've left part of me stuck in the past.

Instead, I focus on the fond memories, the positive aspects, the magic, the fun times, the joy and the happiness we shared. Reclaiming the wholeness I feel when I'm being loving, brings me back to the present and sets ME free to move towards the future in peace, allowing even more of those good things to manifest in my life.

CONFESSION # 39 ...

I KNOW WHAT'S RIGHT FOR ME

I know when something feels good and when it doesn't. I use my own inner guidance to show me.

When I feel inside that something is right for me, I don't need to argue, to get others to agree, to find approval or to prove I'm right ... I just feel the peaceful satisfaction of knowing my own path and allow others the space to discover theirs too.

CONFESSION # 40 ...

I DON'T NEED TO TAKE RISKS

Most times we assume action is what is needed in order to grow, to change what's happening, to get to where we want to go, but, before I start writing, before I make love, before I make a new decision, BEFORE I DO ANYTHING meaningful at all, I line up my energy to be attuned to my creator, to the love inside me, to my own inner guidance ... then the action I take next is inspired, impossible to contain, it seems obvious, compelling and I know completely, that it's the right thing for me.

CONFESSION # 41 ...

I ONLY HAVE ONE WEAKNESS

... criticism makes me more determined,
... feedback makes me grow,
... opposition builds me up,
... controversy is clever advertising,
... but if you really want to get under my skin, "loving me" makes me buckle at the knees.

CONFESSION # 42 ...

I WON'T ASK YOU HOW YOU ARE ... just in case you tell me ... lol

I'd rather know where you're going, who you dream you can become and what you imagine might be the next greatest passion of your entire life.

CONFESSION # 43 ...

CANCER AWARENESS IS ABSURD

Wellness awareness would be a much more life enhancing focus, health consciousness would be a much more impactful goal and affirming the perfection of our own bodies would be a much more fulfilling action.

The greatest healers don't focus on the illness, instead they see us as naturally perfect, whole and complete and their powerful vision brings us into alignment with that profound inner truth.

CONFESSION # 44 …

I WON'T GIVE ADVICE UNLESS YOU ASK FOR IT

… otherwise it's as useless as telling an Atheist that Jesus loves him, buying a book for a blind person, feeding meat to a vegetarian, baking a cake for a super-model, bidding after an auction has ended, convincing a child that vegetables taste great or giving a millionaire $10!

Instead, I just mind my own business and live as an example of what I believe. Actions speak so much louder than words.

CONFESSION # 45 ...

DON'T "EXPECT" ME TO BE FAITHFUL

Being faithful is a demand that's placed on another person to have sex only with their mate.

When faithfulness is offered freely - it is a gift.
When faithfulness is expected - it is control.

Relationships are a place I give my mate freedom to be more of himself, not remove it.

When I feel like I can be ME without any expectations or demands from others, I automatically give my "whole" self to my mate. To me that is the ultimate expression of freedom! Giving something, just because I can.

CONFESSION # 46 ...

I LOVE TO BREAK THE RULES

… it adds so much more passion to life, to love and to a relationship. If you're usually nice, be "dirty", if you tend to be soft, get "tough". Do something different, something dangerous, something "bad". If you often wait, take the initiative. Variety is the spice of life.

CONFESSION # 47 ...

I DON'T FEEL GUILTY ABOUT ANYTHING

Guilt comes from religious teachings - not from God. I prefer to let go of guilt completely and enjoy my fucking life ... lol

CONFESSION # 48 ...

I NEVER COMPROMISE

Compromising is just a quick and dirty way to solve something when both people have to 'trade' in order to get what they want. They're usually forced to make a promise they can't or don't want to keep.

Instead, I celebrate our differences, expect I will grow as a result and revel in finding creative solutions where I stay true to myself and make space for others to do the same.

CONFESSION # 49 ...

I KNOW THE POWER OF WORDS

I think the most powerful words in the universe are "I am" ... closely followed by the word, fuck.

Anything we say after the words "I am" is what we begin to become and fuck is the most versatile word in the English language. Add them all together and we get variations like "Oh dear I think I am fucked!", "I am fucked if I know!", "Gees I am a happy fucker!" but at the moment, I just think that I am fucking incredible!

(If you are wondering why I write this stuff, please refer to CONFESSION # 46 ... I LOVE TO BREAK THE RULES)

CONFESSION # 50 …

THERE ARE SO MANY THINGS I CAN DO

I may not always be able to turn negative energy to positive … but I CAN focus on the positive aspects of what's happening and give more power to that instead.

I CAN find the blessing in every occurrence.
I CAN see the best in my mate and feel better about who we both are.
I CAN remember the fun times and speak about them often.
I CAN appreciate the simple things, like the birds and the bees, the grass and the trees, the rivers and the lakes, the coffee and the cakes.
I CAN imagine a brighter future.
I CAN choose to think about anything that makes me feel good.
I CAN decide to believe that everything always works out in the end.
I CAN cause myself to know, that all things are perfect, just as they are.

CONFESSION # 51 ...

NO ONE IS A BAD PERSON

… there are just some people who are more aligned than others.

Anyone who decides someone else is "bad", that their behaviour is "wrong", that they have committed a "sin", has the same attitude as the person who drops bombs on cities and crashes planes into buildings. Forgive them, for they have no idea how their judgment is making them identical to the very people they are condemning.

CONFESSION # 52 ...

I DON'T TRY TO SOLVE ANYTHING

I just imagine how I'll feel when it's already complete and then allow the solution to find me.

CONFESSION # 53 ...

I MIND MY OWN BUSINESS

When I'm in harmony with my own sense of fulfilment in life, I have no time to judge what another person is doing, no inclination to even look at how others are living, no desire to compare what the next person possesses ... I just tend to my own alignment and add value by being the best example I can possibly be.

CONFESSION # 54 ...

I DON'T CARE WHAT'S GOING ON IN THE WORLD

… I care about my own alignment!

When I feel bad, blame the government, fear natural disasters, worry about wars or criticize major corporations for something that's beyond my control, I've forgotten my own power, leaving me with little energy to give to living.

When I'm in tune with my own alignment, when I'm finding thoughts of hope, when I'm speaking words of encouragement, when I'm performing inspired actions, when I'm having faith and imagining what's possible to create instead, that adds more value to our world and my own life, than I can possibly measure.

CONFESSION # 55 ...

I MAKE MYSELF FEEL BETTER

My goal isn't to find love, success, fulfillment or even joy ... my aim is always to find relief, and I find it in any way I can.

I know that relief for me is often a more positive thought, a quieter moment, a deeper breath or even just a heartbeat away.

CONFESSION # 56 …

I GIVE SO MANY THINGS AWAY

… not because I'm rich and can afford to, not because my parents told me I should, not because you expect me to and not even because I believe it will all come back to me tenfold … I give things away because doing so enriches my human experience, strengthens my feelings of abundance, magnifies the sensation of appreciation for what I've already been given and deeply feeds my soul.

CONFESSION # 57 ...

I MAKE WISE CHOICES

There were times I made terrible decisions ... and the worst decisions are made when I've reacted to something that's happened in the past, to something I'm afraid might happen in the future or to what someone has just said or done.

My best decisions are made when I feel centered, at peace and more connected to the loving person I know I am inside. That's when I choose to take action now ... when my inner wisdom is the easiest to access.

CONFESSION # 58 ...

I'M NOT HERE TO TEACH YOU ANYTHING

… instead, I encourage YOU to trust your own inner knowing, to be guided by the intensity of your feelings, to listen to the calling of your heart, to resonate with the vibration of your soul and decide what your own ideas about a matter will be … Instead of attracting followers, I'd rather inspire leaders!

CONFESSION # 59 ...

I NEVER DISCUSS PROBLEMS

I have learned that it is best to spend only little time defining a problem, no time at all pointing out the cause and all the time in the world brainstorming solutions.

CONFESSION # 60 ...

I ACCEPT YOU AS YOU ARE

I used to try and change other people ... but found it to be a destructive pattern that erodes trust, diminishes respect, reduces passion, fosters dependency, and weakens my ability to influence by choosing to notice only the best in them.

These days I prefer to grow gracefully, be a better example, contribute quietly, explore each person's strengths, find humour, stimulate good feelings, inspire hope, build people up and soothe their souls.

CONFESSION # 61 ...

I CAN BRING OUT THE BEST IN ANYONE

I decided that no matter how the people around me are behaving, I can hold onto my faith in who I know they really are inside and then they pretty soon behave like that instead ... It's always my choice! I have the power to notice the best, to believe in the best, to enhance the best and to bring out the best side of anyone.

CONFESSION # 62 ...

I HAVE NO NEED TO FIGHT

I have no need to fight ... I would lay down my words peacefully so you can feel better.

I have no need to hold grudges ... I would place what's happened in the past and leave it there where it belongs.

I have no need to "be right" about anything at all ... inside my soul lies the truth that holds my integrity intact and leaves you the space to discover your own.

CONFESSION # 63 ...

TODAY IS THE MOST IMPORTANT DAY OF MY LIFE

There's nothing I need to achieve, no records I have to break, no last chance I must take, no great goals to reach, no big deals to make. There's nothing I need to do, but there's something I always choose to "BE" ... I choose to be happy. For in each moment I decide the thoughts to think and the words to say, that make me feel exactly how I do today.

CONFESSION # 64 ...

MY CRITERIA FOR CHOOSING A MATE

... human, breathing & under 500. True!

There's so much good in each one of us that goes unnoticed if my mind is clouded with judgment instead of being curiously intrigued, when I search for excuses NOT to get involved instead of finding more reasons to flow love. I alone hold the key to unlocking my own heart and inviting others to share in the exhilaration of physical, emotional, mental and spiritual intimacy.

CONFESSION # 65 ...

I DON'T GO TO PSYCHICS

They can tell you anything and it can't be disputed. They can advise you to open your Mystic Third Eye, ask if your 21 chakras are fully rotated, predict a massive disturbance in your star quadrant and decide they have the power to open you to natural gifts and talents that might otherwise be unrealized. But what I love the most is that they claim to have transcended the physical plane ... well I've had sex too you know! ... lol

CONFESSION # 66 …

SOMETIMES I SAY STUPID THINGS

… to lighten the mood, to break a negative pattern, to make others laugh, to move some energy and to remind myself that I don't need to have a repertoire, be particularly intelligent or even charming to add value to this world and make someone else smile.

CONFESSION # 67 ...

I STIMULATE THE FEELINGS I ENJOY

I don't watch drama on TV or read the news and only see movies that make me laugh, feel sexy, warm my heart or uplift my spirits. Not because anything else is bad or wrong, but because I care deeply about the way I feel and know it's been one of the greatest contributors to my success.

I choose the flavour of my day by being thoughtful about what I watch, what I read, what I focus on, what I do and what I say.

CONFESSION # 68 ...

THE BEST WAY TO FIX AN UPSET

… is to focus on the other areas of life that don't need fixing. To give more attention to the things that ease my pain, that provide relief, that make me feel better, that inspire hope, that expand my happiness, that lead me to more joy and even greater appreciation for everything I've already been given. What upset? I can't even remember what that was about!

CONFESSION # 69 ...

I HAVE SO MANY THINGS TO APPRECIATE

I've never had to pay for the fresh air that I breathe, the magnificent body I've been given, the rain that waters our planet, the earth with its bountiful riches, the sun that continues to shine, a healthy heart that keeps beating, my incredible mind that keeps expanding. Those things were given freely by a creator who considered us ALL worthy, even before we began.

CONFESSION # 70 ...

ONE DAY I JUST DECIDED TO GIVE UP

... I gave up all struggle,
... I gave up all resistance,
... I gave up all complaining,
... I gave up all contradictory thoughts,
... I gave up all limiting beliefs,
... I gave up all disempowering attitudes,
... I gave up all need to control,
... I gave up wanting other people's approval, permission or understanding and
... I gave up my incessant need to explain or justify who I am, what I'm doing and where I am at.

I NOW ALLOW ... for things to be easy, to go with the flow of life, to think well of myself and others, to only repeat beliefs that give each of us freedom to be who we choose to be, to hold attitudes that serve my expansion, to relax more, to trust my feelings to guide me, to be true to myself, to have faith that everything that occurs is leading me home to an even grander version of love.

CONFESSION # 71 ...

I WROTE MY OWN LIFE STORY

… after realising I'd been accurately acting out a version of my favourite childhood fairytale. So now I'm really living happily-ever-after, attracting each aspect that I consciously choose and even more. But I don't have to put any more thought into it than that … I just decide how I want to feel, entrust the finer details to the universe and just go out and have fun.

CONFESSION # 72 …

I CAN PREDICT YOUR FUTURE

You won't always get what you want, but,

… you'll get what you expect,
… you'll get what you allow,
… you'll get what you focus your attention on,
… you'll get what you believe you are worth,
… you'll also get more of what you are afraid of, what you complain about, worry about and what you have strong emotion about.

AND you'll get so much more of what you truly love and appreciate, because that's the strongest emotion of all.

CONFESSION # 73 ...

THE ONLY TRUTH I EVER LOOK FOR ... is evidence that I am fantastic.

Everything else to the contrary is irrelevant. Seriously!

CONFESSION # 74 ...

I DELIBERATELY SAY THINGS TO MAKE YOU THINK

… to question your beliefs, to reassess your attitude, to clarify your position, to expand your awareness, to inspire new ideas, to interrupt a negative pattern, to make your head spin, to be more conscious about what you are doing, thinking, saying, believing and activating in your current experience of life … and whatever I do for you, I also do for me.

CONFESSION # 75 ...

MY ATTITUDE DETERMINES THE QUALITY OF MY LIFE

I've never been cheated on ... I don't expect anything in return for the love I give.

I've never been ripped off ... I only ever do what I want to do.

I've never been treated badly ... I know that my judgement of your behaviour hurts me more than your actions can ever do.

I've never been deserted ... I don't force someone to keep a promise and never set them free.

I don't even get disappointed ... no one else has to change so I can feel loved, happy and at peace. I give those things to myself as the greatest gift of all.

CONFESSION # 76 ...

LIFE IS SO MUCH EASIER THAN I THOUGHT

One time I thought that something was over and done,
and found out something better had just begun.
Sometimes when my problems seemed too hard to take,
the solution was only a deep breath away.
There were moments when I felt I'd given all I had stored,
then I found the inspiration to give just that little bit more.
When I relax and go with the flow of the stream,
I get taken to more magnificent places than I've ever dreamed.

CONFESSION # 77 ...

I DON'T HAVE PROBLEMS

I just see them as an unexpected challenge, the beginning of a new adventure, the start of something REALLY good, the perfect path to greater abundance/love/health, a blessing in disguise, a surprising twist, an indication that I am about to expand.

Life has no meaning except what I give it ... today I choose a meaning that makes me come alive.

CONFESSION # 78 ...

I DON'T SET MATERIAL GOALS ANYMORE

Once I discovered that the real reason we set goals is NOT for what we think we'll accomplish, not for the experience of reaching them, not even for the gift we'll receive in the end, but for the emotion we think we'll feel when it is all said and done... and if I just imagine that feeling NOW, the goal is already achieved, then there's more time to go out and really enjoy my life.

THE ONLY GOALS I EVER SET NOW ... are emotional ones

... (that I'll find ways to be happy, feel empowered, relaxed, free etc.) I can achieve the feeling place of emotional goals almost any time I decide to, by simply thinking about them ... then the material things just come along while I'm out having fun with life, in their own perfect timing, in their own magnetic way.

CONFESSION # 79 ...

I KNOW HOW TO BRING OUT THE BEST IN MY MAN

Women who are wondering where the 'real' men are, have forgotten their own power ... the power to gently nurture, to playfully tease, to overlook imperfections, to acknowledge the finer qualities, to appreciate his efforts, to value what he provides, to find personal peace, to happily inspire and to LOVE the man of their dreams into life.

(Please refer to CONFESSION # 80 for a balanced gender perspective.)

CONFESSION # 80 ...

MY MAN KNOWS HOW TO BRING OUT THE BEST IN ME

Men who keep searching endlessly for a woman with the "right" attributes, have forgotten their own power ... the power to romantically pursue, to fantasize, to discover ways to make a woman shine, to plan, to surprise, to creatively enhance her life, to make her feel cherished, protected, beautiful and adored and to feel proud of who they support her to become.

(If you don't know how to draw out a man's fine qualities, please refer to CONFESSION # 79 to make it a creative reality with the one you already have.)

CONFESSION # 81 ...

I ATTRACTED MY MATE INTO MY LIFE

I imagined you for an eternity, from deep inside my mind. I watched you soundly sleeping with your heart right next to mine. I walked across the water your hungry soul to seek, as if by chance I'd see you there, my body craving for us to meet.

But I wanted YOU to find me; it was something I did ask. My searching felt so frustrating and not a woman's task. I thank God you heard me calling bringing sunshine to my eyes, and paved the way for us to meet with such a sweet surprise.

Your voice so recognizable I knew without a doubt ... we talked as if forever had known us inside out. Now that I can sense you, so intimately by my side, I want to savour these precious moments anticipation cannot hide.

There have been one thousand angels who've conspired to draw us near. They felt the longing of my soul and knew the crying of my tears. Your lips were made to catch them, my pining heart to calm, and your arms were made to hold me and protect me from all harm.

You might wonder what I've done to you; I've called you from afar, the heavens caused the earth to move the sun the moon and stars. For us to be together the time has finally come, and when we look into each other's eyes, we know that we are home.

CONFESSION # 82 ...

I DON'T KNOW WHAT'S RIGHT FOR YOU

While I might appreciate my clarity of mind, it may be appropriate for you to be growing through confusion. While I might be enjoying comfort and stability, you may feel the need to move and expand. While I might value the finer things in life, you may be happier with simplicity.

I no longer assume I know what's best for anyone.

CONFESSION # 83 ...

I KNOW HOW I CREATE MY OWN REALITY

When I think something is too good to be true, I am right.

When I wonder if something else might be possible, I am open.

When I decide it's time to suspend past beliefs, I am shifting.

When I hope that something I dream of will come true, I am guided.

When I believe that everything always works out for me, I am shown.

When I know I can attract anything I desire, I create my own reality.

CONFESSION # 84 ...

I STOPPED COMPARING MYSELF TO OTHER PEOPLE

Instead, I decided to love my life just the way it is, to love my mate just the way he is and especially to love myself just the way I am ... there's a tremendous feeling of satisfaction in deciding that.

CONFESSION # 85 ...

I KEEP FEELING BETTER AND BETTER

... with each happy experience I recall, every day I spend doing whatever I feel like, in the moment I find something to laugh about, at any time I make peace with where I'm at, with each thought I turn into a positive, with every word I speak that uplifts another, with each new dream I dream and when I do the things that make my inner light shine more vibrantly than ever before.

CONFESSION # 86 ...

I DON'T DO INTERVIEWS

I let the words I write, speak for themselves. All I do is deliver what's inspired, answer questions that are asked and allow solutions to be drawn through me. The rest is guru worship and serves no higher purpose. I prefer you worship your own intuition; you adore finding your own alignment, you love creating your own material ... and let the world be enhanced even more by your presence in it.

CONFESSION # 87 ...

I CAN PROCRASTINATE

Procrastination is a label we use to describe when something doesn't feel quite right but we assume that taking ACTION is more important than feeling aligned with what we're doing. I make sure my heart and my mind are in harmony with what I desire to achieve before I get out of bed before I make a new decision or before I take any action at all.

CONFESSION # 88 ...

I AM RESOURCEFUL

While most people think they need money to survive ... I rely on "resourcefulness" more than anything else.

I can entertain people and get attention. I can write a book and feel important. I can quieten my mind and experience bliss. I can be myself and feel free. I can use my imagination to travel anywhere I want. I can collect veges from the garden and cook up a feast ... OR I can stop for a moment, feel my wholeness, acknowledge that "I am enough", and let it deeply feed my soul.

CONFESSION # 89 ...

I CAN GET WHAT I WANT IN AN INSTANT

... by giving it to someone else.

If I want to receive love, I share love.
If I want to be understood, I take time to understand another point of view.
If I want to feel wealthy, I give away something that someone else can use more.
If I want to feel free, I let something I've been holding onto, go.
If I want acknowledgment, I acknowledge someone else.
If I want to be accepted just as I am, I accept myself first, and then make what anyone else thinks, completely irrelevant.

We only want things because we think it will make us "feel better". Giving does NOT mean we'll receive, but it does re-stimulate the natural flow of energy! I love the power of not expecting others to give me what I need and give it to myself instead ... and they thrive on the freedom to choose.

CONFESSION # 90 ...

I DON'T EXPECT ANYTHING IN RETURN

... for the love I give, for the things I do, for the care I show, for the joy I bestow. I do things because they are a natural expression of who I really am. The more I do things because they make ME feel good, the more aligned I feel, the better others around me feel and the closer we get to experiencing the joy, love and freedom that is the basic desire of each of us.

CONFESSION # 91 ...

PAIN DOESN'T MOTIVATE ME

It just makes me feel bad ... but I do use it as a reference point to realise when I need to focus in a different direction. Relief, positivity, peace, pleasure, passion, fun, love, laughter, beauty, bliss, ease, ecstasy and exhilaration are forever calling me to enjoy them ... and when I take the time to remember what they feel like, I am gently transported to where they reside ... inside my soul.

CONFESSION # 92 ...

I STARTED TO REALLY LIVE

... the moment I stopped caring what my parents, what my kids, what my mate or what YOU might think of me. What a wonderful adventure it is to joyously explore the deepest parts of my own soul ... to remember that your opinion of me is a reflection of your own state of mind ... and that my exploration is a reflection of my commitment to choose integrity over conformity, any day!

CONFESSION # 93 …

THERE ARE TIMES I WILL IGNORE YOU COMPLETELY

… when what you are doing or saying causes discomfort. Instead I just focus on the parts of you that bring me comfort instead. That doesn't mean what you are doing or saying is wrong, it just means it doesn't resonate with who I know inside we both really are.

The alignment with my soul is far more important, than my judgment of your behaviour will ever be.

CONFESSION # 94 ...

I DON'T TRY TO MOTIVATE MYSELF

MOTIVATION IS when I get hold of an idea because I think it will make me feel a certain way, and then make an effort to carry it through to its logical conclusion.

INSPIRATION IS when an idea gets hold of me because I've accessed the feelings I really wanted to feel anyway, and it takes me effortlessly to where I intended to go in the first place.

CONFESSION # 95 ...

I'M ALREADY SUCCESSFUL

Success isn't something I achieve at the end of a journey! I feel incredibly successful each day as I relax my worries, tend to my happiness, do what I love to do ... and then watch as amazing opportunities are presented, tasks are done with a sense of delight and everything unfolds effortlessly along the way.

CONFESSION # 96 ...

THE KEY TO A HAPPY LIFE

... isn't to manipulate the conditions around me so I can feel better, the key is to change the "meaning" I give it and feel happy no matter what happens.

CONFESSION # 97 ...

LIFE IS WHAT I MAKE IT

No one needs a life-coach, a therapist, a library of books, endless study material, a guru, a seminar or anything else to enjoy life to its fullest. I was NOT meant to struggle, to strive, to fight for my place, to work hard, to face fears, to do it tough ... life is meant to be fun, to feel good and be enjoyed.

CONFESSION # 98 ...

I DON'T CARE IF OTHER PEOPLE LOVE ME

When I am so attuned, so happy, so connected to my own soul, it doesn't matter how other people are behaving. I KNOW how good it feels to flow the natural love that's bursting inside me. It gives me more pleasure and power to love myself first, than what I get from waiting for other people to give it to me. When I'm happy with who I am being, it adds more value to our world than I'll ever know!

I know WHO I AM and who other people are being is their own business - not mine.

CONFESSION # 99 ...

I FOUND THE SECRET TO PERFECT HEALTH

It's not about what I do; it's about HOW I FEEL while I'm doing it.

That's why people who feel guilty about smoking can be stricken with lung cancer and others can smoke happily until the day they die. Illness is not a random occurrence. It stems from my emotions (fear of death and dying), my thoughts (that illness is a bad thing), my beliefs (as I get older I expect to get weaker) and with my words (I'm sick and tired). But it can shift in an instant, by doing whatever it takes to find relief from the discomfort ... and to allow my natural state of ease and comfort to run the show instead.

I FOUND THE SECRET TO PERFECT WEIGHT

It's not about what I eat; it's about HOW I FEEL while I'm eating it.

I FOUND THE SECRET TO A PERFECT LIFE

It's not about how I live; it's about HOW I FEEL while I'm living it. I'm thoroughly enjoying mine!

CONFESSION #100 …

I DISCOVERED A WAY TO STAY HAPPY MOST OF THE TIME

I simply relax OR I focus my mind on things that make me feel good … and I don't communicate, I don't write, I don't make decisions, I don't express it to others if I feel bad.

I get over it, through it, move around it or past it FIRST. In this way I give less emphasis to the things I don't want and activate more of the things that I do … I love knowing that!

CONFESSION #101 ...

MIRACLES HAPPEN SO OFTEN IN MY WORLD

... that they're not miracles anymore, they're just another beautiful part of life. I've gotten better at noticing them, attracting them, expecting them and deeply appreciating them.

It's natural for my body to heal when I focus on wellness, it's natural for my weight to balance when I focus on happiness, it's natural for life to go well when I focus on what's already working, it's natural for money to flow if I'm focused on what I love to do. Being alive is the greatest miracle of all! It's a miracle I've written this many confessions ... lol

(Those who have created their own "miracles" by defying a medical prognosis, overcoming allergies, creating ease from disease or living through a seemingly terminal condition, understand more fully their own power of focus. That finding joy, laughing, ignoring negativity, having faith, being hopeful and living their dreams have a more profound impact on restoring their natural healthy state, than seeking a cure will ever accomplish.)

CONFESSION #102 ...

I KNOW HOW TO GET WHAT I WANT

Some people take action, some use visualization,
some people pray, some just don't know any way.
But for me, I relax and I flow with the stream,
and have faith that what's happening will show me my dream.

But my dream isn't a bigger house,
or to have more success,
it isn't money or love or even to do my best.
It's simply to comprehend fully, how much I've already been blessed.

(I've set the wheels in motion, now it's time to sit back and enjoy the ride.)

CONFESSION #103 ...

WHAT OTHERS CHOOSE IS NONE OF MY BUSINESS

It doesn't matter how my mate, employees or children are choosing to live their lives! If it doesn't feel "right" to me I readjust my perception, release my judgment or remove myself from the situation. Trying to change other people is futile. My greatest power is to live in integrity with my own beliefs and give my actions an opportunity to show other people, another way to thrive.

CONFESSION #104 ...

I'M A PRETENDER

I never wait for things to happen. I pretend they're already here. Then I have all the time in the world to appreciate the simple things, like taking a calming deep breath, listening to the happy laughter of children, smelling the deliciousness of freshly brewed coffee.

(We only want certain things because we think they'll make us feel good! When we feel good in the moment, what we want has already arrived.)

CONFESSION #105 ...

I DO WHAT'S RIGHT FOR ME

I used to think it was appropriate to just say "no", but I've stopped doing that and instead, I just let go!

I used to think it was proper to fight for what is right, but I've stopped pointing out the dark and instead, I've turned more towards the light.

I used to think it was best to ask others to change their ways, but I've stopped expecting them to make me happy, instead, I just remember better days.

I was taught by my elders the way that I should be, but now I've found out for myself, it best to do what's right for me!

CONFESSION #106 ...

IT'S MY JOB TO FIND HAPPINESS - IT'S NOT YOUR JOB TO GIVE IT TO ME!

Every time I find peace with my thoughts - I grow my mind
Every time I accept who you are and find happiness anyway - I expand my heart.
Every time I flow love because it is who I really am inside - I connect to my soul.
Every time I do this for me without expecting anything of you - I profoundly add value to the life of all.

CONFESSION #107 ...

NO ONE CAN EVER ARGUE WITH ME

I don't give their words any power. Instead I remember the wonderful things that happened in the past. I think about how much I appreciate them in the present. I talk about how I dream of better things in the future OR I am silent and hold the vision of those things so strongly in my imagination that the strength of their issue dissipates with every word they utter.

CONFESSION #108 ...

IT'S NO SURPRISE TO ME THAT YOU'RE DOING INCREDIBLY WELL

I believed in you right from the start. I knew you were more than you were pretending to be. I saw the strength of your spirit and felt the power of your intense desire - to have more, do more and be more than you already are.

It's the desire that started the ball rolling, it's your decision to follow it that moved you forward, it's your belief that anything is possible, that kept the momentum going. It's your faith in the power of the universe that's brought you right here right now, to this very profound moment, where you can KNOW that what you've asked for, is already completely and utterly done!

CONFESSION #109 ...

MY GREATEST ACCOMPLISHMENTS

… have nothing to do with money I've made, success I've achieved, respect I've earned.

The BEST achievements were when I opened my heart just that little bit more despite how someone else was behaving, when I kept expanding my mind to understand a different point of view no matter what someone else was saying, when I decided a situation would benefit me far more than it could ever hinder my progress.

CONFESSION #110 ...

I'M NO WISER THAN YOU

I'm just able to access infinite intelligence easily as I become more closely aligned with my own sense of self.

Everyone has their OWN inner wisdom. Some express it by making movies, creating art, cooking a meal, sharing a smile, writing a song, inspiring growth, teaching a craft, making us laugh, being happy, giving encouragement, uplifting another.

You are much wiser than you think!

CONFESSION #111 ...

I HAVE A VIVID IMAGINATION

I imagine sick people as well, depressed people as happy. I imagine those who complain of having no money appreciating what they already have, those who seek a relationship finding the company of their own soul. I imagine those who feel lost beginning to trust their own guidance, those who are worried remembering deep inner peace ... and then I call them towards the vision I clearly know is who they really are.

CONFESSION #112 ...

I USED TO LOOK FOR FAULTS IN OTHERS ... so I could feel superior and separate.

Now I look for their magnificence, so I can see my reflection and bring us all closer.

CONFESSION #113 ...

TODAY I'M GOING ON A TREASURE HUNT

... to find nuggets of happiness in the most simple activities,
... to dive for pearls of wisdom in the even the most mundane conversations,
... to look for diamonds of joy in the actions of people around me and
... to see jewels of the divine rising from each person's soul.

CONFESSION #114 ...

I'VE PUT THE LIFE BACK INTO DEATH

Instead of pretending I'm sad when someone I know dies, I choose to celebrate the life that they've lived.
Instead of mourning the loss of someone I love, I look forward to the deeper spiritual connection I'm about to enjoy.
Instead of believing that death is a curse, I've decided to count it as one of my blessings.
Instead of being afraid of the unknown, I cherish the thought of taking a new adventure.
Instead of assuming it's the ending of life, I expect it will be the expansion of my soul.
Instead of living cautiously as if death is the enemy, I decided to live life fully and know that heaven is my friend.

I know heaven exists, and it lives in my heart, connected by my mind to the depths of my eternal soul.

CONFESSION #115 ...

I ALWAYS FEEL ABUNDANTLY WEALTHY

... when I take the time to appreciate what I've already been given.

WHILE MOST PEOPLE SET MATERIAL, FINANCIAL OR SUCCESS ORIENTATED GOALS

... I set emotional goals! I know that having more stuff, reaching a business milestone or receiving an award makes me feel good temporarily, but the only reason I set those goals is because I think they'll make me feel good in the end ... and if I do whatever it takes to feel good NOW, my goal is already achieved, instantly!

CONFESSION #116 ...

I LOVE TO EXAGGERATE

I emphasise everything that feels good and minimise anything that doesn't. I talk incessantly about what makes my heart sing, I bask endlessly in the fullness of my own creativity, I loudly amplify my appreciation for the perfection of life, I dramatize boldly the stories of happy times and expand further on whatever inspires hope, understanding, comfort, peace, freedom, delight and joy.

CONFESSION #117 ...

THINGS ARE SO MUCH BETTER THAN I EVER EXPECTED

In the moment I wish for something to be different, I know it is already in the process of becoming real. But my job isn't to set goals and make it happen, my job is to align with my creator and allow even more things than I can possibly remember that I've asked for, to occur at the right time, with the best people, in the most magnificent ways, in moments of complete and utter divine perfection.

CONFESSION #118 ...

I LOVE AND APPRECIATE ALL MY EX'S

… and wouldn't dream of defying my natural loving nature to hate the very person who has been the greatest catalyst, that made me expand into who I've become today.

CONFESSION #119 ...

I NEVER NEED TO PROMOTE MY SERVICES

I just stop and appreciate each chance I've ever been given, have great fun doing whatever turns me on at the time, get "in sync" with my dream and marvel as the most fabulous clients, the most amazing people and the most incredible opportunities are magnetised to me like bees to pollen, like actors to a stage, like lovers who were inside each other all along.

CONFESSION #120 ...

WHEN TIMES ARE TOUGH ... I'm determined to fly higher, so that when times are good ... I soar!

CONFESSION #121 ...

SOMETIMES, "BEING CONFUSED" IS A REALLY GOOD PLACE TO BE

When my mind is scrambled, I have no choice but to "turn to my heart" for comfort, to remember peace, to receive the clearest guidance. I have always found it to be the beginning of a major breakthrough. "To every thing there is a season, and a time for every purpose under heaven".

CONFESSION #122 ...

THERE ARE THREE WAYS I CAN RESPOND TO SITUATIONS

1. ... as if things just happen and my response to them is out of my control.

2. ... as if things just happen and my response to them is based on how other people think I should respond, on how other people have responded in the past, on what society thinks is the "appropriate" response in each situation.

3. ... as if things just happen and I can choose what I will focus on, I can influence the way I respond, I decide what it all means, I mold my own beliefs and create the life of MY dreams.

CONFESSION #123 ...

I MADE A DISCOVERY

What I appreciate today, multiplies tomorrow.
What I think about today, determines the quality of tomorrow.
What I talk about today expands tomorrow.
What I complain about today magnifies tomorrow.
What I focus on today has the ability to make or break the future I dream myself having, so I'm choosing a good one!

CONFESSION #124 …

IT DOESN'T MATTER WHAT I BELIEVE … I always get to be right.

It doesn't matter what I think … it always effects my emotions.
I doesn't matter what I say … it always influences my attitude.
I doesn't matter what I do … when I align my thoughts, beliefs and attitudes with what I really want, then I become more conscious of my own power, to weave the fibre of life in my own unique fashion.

CONFESSION #125 ...

DON'T EXPECT ME TO BE NICE

If you need others to be nice so you can feel good, then you never have an opportunity to claim your own power ... the power to "KNOW WHO YOU ARE" no matter how someone else is behaving. Instead of being weak and becoming dependent, I encourage you to find your own alignment and uncover what empowerment really is.

CONFESSION #126 ...

I DON'T NEED YOU TO CHANGE

If my level of happiness depends on YOU changing, I am enslaved for a lifetime.
If my level of happiness depends on ME changing, I am free forevermore.

CONFESSION #127 ...

SOME THINGS ARE BETTER LEFT UNSAID

I've learned that it is better to only speak of things I want to experience more of, so ...

... I no longer complain about what isn't right, I'm thankful for what is.

... I don't tell someone what I don't like, I acknowledge what I do.

... I don't talk about the problems, instead I reach for resolutions.

... I don't magnify what I don't have, but appreciate everything, especially you!

CONFESSION #128 …

THE ONLY TIME I EVER FEEL DISCONTENT

… is when I look for something outside myself to fulfill a feeling I want on the inside.

Another relationship won't really make me feel more loved.
A bigger house won't really make me feel more prosperous.
A better job won't really make me feel more successful.
The ability to control my circumstances won't really make me feel more secure.
Going on another holiday won't really make me feel more free.

When I allow myself to feel those feelings from the inside first, the outside details become irrelevant, and more appropriate results occur in perfect natural timing … just as if they were waiting for me to relax and receive them all along.

CONFESSION #129 ...

I LOVE MANY THINGS

Sometimes I attach the feeling of love to other people, a piece of art, a particular song, a place, an imaginary person, a home, a pet, a child, a movie character.

But I don't really love those other things at all!

I am loving what I THINK they are,
I am loving who I IMAGINE them to be,
I am loving the feeling I get when I FLOW my love no matter where it's directed!

So what's really happening is that I am loving ME, I am being ME and I am expressing who I know inside I really am …

… and when I am loving me, other people feel it and fall in love too.

CONFESSION #130 ...

I'VE CHOSEN MY FUTURE

I am destined to have a fabulous life full of exciting adventure, endless love, great success and blissful happiness.

Now, when I relax and stop thinking those thoughts, having those conversations and doing those things that prevent me from experiencing what I've always dreamed of, they come floating towards me in the most perfect moment and I'll say, "I remember you ... thanks for always being there, waiting endlessly for me!"

CONFESSION #131 ...

I'M A CREATOR

I don't complain about my current reality - I create the one I want by pretending things are better than they seem to be, by imagining a brighter tomorrow, by faking it 'till I make it and by having such a strong vision of what's possible, that it can do nothing else but become real.

CONFESSION #132 ...

I AM ALWAYS TAKEN CARE OF

No matter where I go I am always wrapped in the welcoming arms of friends, neighbours and even strangers. When asking for help I often sense a "divine energy" gently showing me what I was asking to see, softly giving me the answers that I so wanted to hear, peacefully guiding my footsteps to where I am best to go ... and it comforts me more than words can say.

CONFESSION #133 ...

SOMETIMES MY THOUGHTS DRIVE ME NUTS

... and that's the time I need to distract myself and do something else ... like go for a walk, take a nap, dance to loud music or meditate and STOP the current train of thought for a while. Good things flow to me so naturally, that all I have to do is get my mind out of the way, relax and allow them to occur. It's so much easier that you think!

(If I want to change what I'm thinking about quickly, moving my body shifts my focus and changes my thoughts.)

CONFESSION #134 ...

I HAVE VERY HIGH STANDARDS FOR A RELATIONSHIP

But the standards I set are for MY behaviour, not for my mate.

I intend to flow as much love and appreciation towards him as I can, not because he deserves it, not because I feel obligated, not because I'm supposed to, not even because I made a promise, but because it feels like heaven to flow divine loving energy from my inside out and be even more of who I really am.

CONFESSION #135 ...

I FIND STRENGTH IN VULNERABILITY

... to ask for help when I need it without expecting it to come in a particular way, to tenderly nurture the little girl inside me who just wants to curl up and be loved for ALL of who she is, to soothe my own soul through the tears, to make peace with the inner turmoil, to reach for the comforting hand of my creator ... and sense the perfection of it all!

CONFESSION #136 ...

I FAKE IT UNTIL I MAKE IT

… by assuming a new identity and creating a more expanded version of who I already am.

I remember the moment I decided to be a writer, a sensual goddess, a photographer, an uplifter, a fabulous parent, a powerful creator, a magnificent lover, a best-selling author. No one else ever needs to approve it, to agree with it or to even like it … I am what I declare myself to be … and I let no one sway me from my belief and knowing that it's already true!

CONFESSION #137 ...

I DON'T HAVE ANY PROBLEMS

... and if I did, I wouldn't broadcast them to the world. I stay silent, stay calm, stay centred and let them pass by easily. The solution is always found when I stop complaining about the issue and when I stop describing the pain, when I stop activating the very thing I want to get rid of.

CONFESSION #138 ...

I'M SO GRATEFUL THAT GOD GAVE ME A CLITORIS

... in fact, I'm really grateful God created orgasm too. I'm incredibly grateful I have the freedom to speak about subjects that are considered taboo, and I am also grateful that "the God I know" has a sense of humour and accepts me just the way I am.

CONFESSION #139 ...

I DON'T CARE HOW LONG A RELATIONSHIP LASTS

… all I care about is the quality I add to each moment, that I am being true to my own desires, that I live in integrity with my beliefs, that I give everything I have to give, including speaking my mind, opening my heart wider and doing what feels right for me.

I don't live with regrets - I live and love with passion.

CONFESSION #140 ...

I CAN HAVE A RELATIONSHIP WITH ALMOST ANYONE

While most people look for a mate who is compatible, who will love them, who will give them what they need, I choose to enter a relationship when most of my needs are already met and I have an abundance of "me" to give.

I am true to myself no matter what others might be thinking,

I focus on the best attributes of each person no matter what they might be saying,

I find happiness no matter what else might be happening,

... and the right one comes along, no effort at all!

CONFESSION #141 ...

I LIVE IN A DREAM

I'm the star, the director, the producer, the scriptwriter and the leading character all rolled into one.

While you might live in the real world - I choose to live in fantasy land, where happiness, bliss and euphoria abound, everything I desire is created in my imagination and sooner or later ALL my dreams come true.

(Years ago, people wished they could get thinner without having to diet, get bigger muscles without needing to exercise, fly in the sky without being a bird, go to the moon without having to dream, talk to people in others countries without it costing the world --- seems like those fantasies have now become reality too.)

CONFESSION #142 ...

I LIKE TO GIVE PEOPLE HOPE

to help them to feel safe,
let them know they are loved,
spread some good news,
lift them up, make them laugh,
tell a happy story,
remember what I like about them,
pay a compliment,
think about their best side,
share an inspiring vision,
fall in love, set them free ...

... and what I do for others, I also do for ME.

CONFESSION #143 ...

HAPPINESS IS MY FOUNTAIN OF YOUTH

... the elixir of life, the placebo for the mind, the philosophers stone and the way of the future. It's free to generate, doesn't need to be stored, packed away or saved for a rainy day. It can be expressed in any moment, sought in each situation and found in any event. Noticing things to be happy about gives life purpose, attracts others and connects me to all that exists, in the deepest way!

CONFESSION #144 ...

HOME IS WHERE I FEEL THE MOST ALIGNED

... and at peace, at one, in heaven, in love, living for each moment, loving with all our hearts, connecting through the tingling sensation of touch, stimulating conversation with insightful minds, expressing the deepest emotions, feeling life energy flow through each cell of our bodies, knowing our creator is joining with us in joyous celebration of lives well lived.

CONFESSION #145 ...

THE SUN ALWAYS COMES UP TOMORROW

The desire "to be loved" is stronger than "the need to be right". Mother Nature always adapts. Living with passion is more enticing than being afraid. Giving love, feels so much better than expecting it. I continually evolve towards the light. The notion of a loving God is more powerful than the story of a vengeful father. My soul is forever calling me home!

CONFESSION #146 ...

I CAN CHANGE MY MOOD

It's just as easy to focus on something that makes me feel good, than on something that makes me feel bad. It's just as easy to praise others as it is to criticize them. It's just as easy to imagine a wonderful future as it is to remember the problems of the past. It's just as easy to laugh about someone who annoys me as it is to get angry with them ... and it feels so much better too!

CONFESSION #147 ...

I ENJOY MULTIPLE ORGASMS

... that have little to do with my partner and everything to do with the way I prepare my body, mind and soul, nurturing myself with beauty treats, romantic movies, sensual dance and speaking from the heart etc.

Things that relax me into my soft feminine energy do more for intimate relationships than anything else!

CONFESSION #148 ...

I AM ALWAYS TRUE TO MYSELF ... no exceptions!

My determined intention to be who I really am (without needing permission, approval or acceptance) creates miracles and unlocks doors, produces magic and lights the way, it opens the floodgates of heaven, attracts cooperative people and awakens me to opportunities, blessings and insights I might never have seen, heard, sensed or even felt, if I was trying to follow someone else's idea for my life!

CONFESSION #149 ...

I NEVER WISH FOR THINGS TO BE DIFFERENT

I just decide to find hope, to know myself better, to view the beauty, to feel delight, to express appreciation, to find reasons to be happy, to see perfection, to experience ecstasy, to search for the blessings, to choose an empowering meaning, to be in total joy and to know peace in every situation that occurs.

CONFESSION #150 ...

I AM WEALTHY BEYOND MY WILDEST DREAMS ... in all ways!

And the part that feels the most fulfilling is the richness contained in my spirit. To me, real wealth is about what I'd have left if all my money, all my possessions and all my connections were gone. I'd still have an abundance of love to give, a prosperous mind, the creativity to make my own fortune, the treasure of an intimate relationship with my source, pure gold in knowing who I really am ... and that's worth far more than money, power, position and possessions can ever buy!

CONFESSION #151 ...

FALLING IN LOVE IS A DECISION ... to open my heart to another.

CHEMISTRY IS STIMULATED BY AN OPEN MIND ... which triggers an emotionally charged thought previously conceived in the imagination.

STAYING IN LOVE IS A CHOICE ... to keep using my imagination to open my heart and mind and focus on the wonderful things that made falling in love so divine.

CONFESSION #152 …

SOMETIMES I'M WRONG!

CONFESSION #153 ...

I CAN'T CHANGE OTHER PEOPLE

... so I never waste time or energy trying to manipulate them into giving me what I want. The reality is, I only want things because I think it will make me feel better. When I choose to simply focus on things that do feel better, it gives me what I want immediately ... the rest is attracted to me, inspired from inside and guided by forces greater than I can fathom.

CONFESSION #154 ...

SOMETIMES I WONDER IF I'VE DIED AND GONE TO HEAVEN!

I work harder now that I've ever done in my life, doing what makes me feel totally alive, following my bliss, aligning with my creator ... and it feels like pleasure, it comes from pure inspiration and it gives me more joy that I could have ever imagined possible.

CONFESSION #155 ...

I LOVE MY PERKY BREASTS ... the shape of my feminine body, my long natural hair.

I love knowing the incredible power of my mind and feeling the warmth that exudes from my heart.

Too often we speak ill of ourselves ... Stop doing that! It's now time to see yourself better, not by talking about what YOU think is the current truth about you, but by telling the truth of how our creator knows you really are. Perfect!

CONFESSION #156 ...

MY BELIEFS CAN CHANGE OVERNIGHT

In the instant I realise a belief no longer serves me, it is replaced with something new, something stimulating, something heartwarming, something life affirming ... and this too could change!

CONFESSION #157 ...

NO ONE SHOULD EVER WANT TO BE LIKE ME

... you should only ever want to be MORE like you!

You have a unique character, special traits, deep insight, amazing passion. You have great power, internal guidance and freedom to choose. No one can sculpt your life as superbly as you and if you've previously given it away to parents, to your mate or some guru ... it's time to claim it back and choose anew.

You are of great value to this world.

CONFESSION #158 ...

INSTEAD OF SPEAKING MY MIND ... I prefer to speak from the heart!

CONFESSION #159 ...

I DO WHATEVER MAKES ME FEEL GOOD

... even if it means not doing anything at all and just being totally in the moment, finding the best thought that brings relief, imagining an exciting virtual reality, sending a message expressing love, noticing each spine-tingling sensation, raising my hands to the sky in deep appreciation for all that I have, all that I am and all I am about to become.

CONFESSION #160 ...

I DON'T WASTE A SECOND OF MY DAY

… trying to work out why someone else is behaving a certain way or what I'll do to try and fix it.

Instead, I use my time to relax back into this moment, to feel more intimately the guidance given by my feelings and move closer to the powerful source of life itself. It's then I'm able to impact those around me in the most profound way, just by being present!

CONFESSION #161 …

MY GOLDEN RULE … I choose to love.

CONFESSION #162 ...

THE ONLY THING I ASK OF YOU ... is that you listen to the guidance from your heart and feel the freedom to choose what is right for you!

Anything else I have ever asked of you has come from a place of misalignment, of forgetting how to meet my own needs, make myself happy, bring myself comfort, give myself peace. But when I am aligned I need nothing else, for your presence in my life is the greatest gift of all.

CONFESSION #163 ...

I ALWAYS EXPECT GOOD THINGS TO HAPPEN

... that everything will work out even better than I imagine ... that miracles are not only possible, but more than likely ... that instead of moving backwards, I am simply moving on ... that wonderful delights are on their way to me right now ... and that I am about to experience more joy, more freedom, more peace and more love than ever before.

CONFESSION #164 ...

I DON'T CARE WHAT OTHER PEOPLE THINK

Have you ever noticed that it doesn't matter how hard we try to please other people, they're rarely satisfied?

When I gave up wondering what others might think about me, I stopped worrying about how I'd look, I stopped being afraid of their reaction, I stopped holding back from doing the things I REALLY wanted to do and seized the opportunity to freely express my "real personality" ... and found it to be one of the greatest gifts I have to give ... to God, to my family, my mate and to the world!

CONFESSION #165 ...

MY SOUL IS CALLING ME ...

... to remember I have everything I need right now
... to know that I am enough
... to believe I am worth it
... to trust the power of my deepest desires
... to allow myself time to feel my inner guidance
... to move forward when inspiration propels me there
... to have faith in the love we all have inside
... to say YES to what I really want
... to be true to myself
... to feel my alignment with the peace inside me
... to relax and float gently along with the current of pleasurable, joyful, ease and abundance.

CONFESSION #166 ...

I CAN HAVE ANYTHING MY HEART DESIRES

I imagine it, think about it, talk about it, write about it, begin to believe it and before long, I know it ... and then it all just happens. There's nothing that can ever stop me except the story I keep telling. When I change the story, I change the result.

CONFESSION #167 ...

SOMETIMES I LOVE BEING RIGHT!

CONFESSION #168 ...

WHILE MOST PEOPLE TRY TO AVOID HAVING PROBLEMS ... I welcome them.

Without hell, there would be no heaven. Without a problem, there would be no solutions. Without questions there would be no answers. Without eternal challenges, there would be no reason on earth to grow.

If I'm feeling sad, I go out of my way to find happiness.

If I can't pay my bills, I look for methods to create more money.

If I'm feeling sick and tired, I come up with a solution to feel better and energized.

If I want my freedom, I stop pretending that I don't already have it ;-)

CONFESSION #169 ...

EVERYTHING ON EARTH IS HERE FOR US TO USE

I use these gifts to enhance my experience of life, not to detract from it.

Use drugs to make you feel alive, not as an escape from life.
Use sex as a way to experience the depth of your feelings, not as a tool to change someone else's.
Use depression to explore the reason for your existence, not as a reason to cease to exist.
Use obesity as a way to be proud and show individuality, not as a cover up of your true identity.
Use food as a way to nourish your body, not as a way to abuse your soul.
Use alcohol as a way to drink in life's riches, not as a way to lose your richness of life.
Use money to add pleasure to your experiences, not as the only way you experience pleasure.
Use personality to make other people feel good, instead of just making yourself feel good.
Use gossip to lift people up, not to "bring them down".
Use Facebook as a place to create long term relationships, not as a place to enlist the most followers.
Use cigarettes as a means to choose your own death consciously, not as a way to pretend you are unconscious.
Use addictions to discover the positive intent behind your actions, not as a way to define your identity.
Use wealth to inspire a life of purpose, not as the only purpose of life.
Use rape as a way to passionately love someone, not as a way to violently hurt them.

Use anger as a path to claim your own power, not as a path to power over others.
Use fear as something to rise above, not as something that rises above you.
Use habits to build a solid foundation for your life, not as the scapegoat for poor choices.
Use your mind to expand your horizons, not as a way to limit your potential.
Use words to convey your own truth, not as a way to change the truth of others.
Use actions to demonstrate the magnificent creature you are, not to demonstrate a low self-image.
Use religion to unite the world with one message, not to cause confusion with many.
Use attitude to express "who you really are", not just who you THINK you are.
Use your beliefs to show how tolerant you can be, not as a way to show inflexibility.
Use loud music as a way to enhance your life, not as a way to detract from the life of others.
Use cosmetic surgery as a way to start a new future, not as a way to return to the past.
Use television as a way to experience entertainment, not as a way to experience life.
Use the news as leverage for change, not as a forgone conclusion.
Use the past to cultivate a garden of blessings, not as a place to dig up rotten carcasses.
Use pain to lead you in a different direction, not to hold on to and stay where you are.
Use your partner as if they are the greatest gift, not as if they owe you a favour.
Use heart-break to remember you've experienced great love, not as an excuse to close down your feelings.
Use your children as the catalyst to practice unconditional love, not as if they need to give reasons to be worthy of your love.

Use abortion as a way to remove distress, not as a way to replace carelessness.

Use marriage as a way to allow your mate greater freedom to be themselves, not as a way to remove their choice.

Use right and wrong to define your OWN path, not as a way to define the path of others.

Use peace to create freedom inside yourself, not as something you fight for in order to obtain.

Use war as a way to seek better resolutions, not as a way to force a solution.

Use business to break down international barriers, not to build more walls.

Use euthanasia to promote free will, not as a way to remove choice.

Use meditation as a way to view the world as "one", not as a way to make yourself superior.

Use exercise as a way to experience health on all levels, not as a way to display an obsession.

Use cancer and disease as a springboard to change, not as something you struggle with in order to stay the same.

Use age to grow in wisdom, not to shrink in dissatisfaction.

Use faith to change YOUR SELF, not to change others.

Use knowledge to teach others to be teachers, not simply to attract the most students.

Use wisdom to leave a legacy for the future, not as something you keep to yourself.

Use love to change the world … and to know it as perfect … just the way it is … that you are perfect … just the way you are … that everything happens at the right time and for the right reasons … for nothing is ever truly right or wrong OR good or bad, unless you declare it so.

CONFESSION #170 ...

EACH PERSON FINDS THEIR OWN ANSWERS - THESE ARE SIMPLY MINE

I care not if people are unaware of the light-hearted humour contained in them, challenge them, disagree with them or simply don't understand them. All I care about is my alignment, feeling uplifted, living my truth and being in integrity with what I know feels right to me.

CONFESSION #171 ...

THERE'S NOTHING I NEED TO FIX

Problems always seem bigger when I'm out of alignment, when I'm feeling "off", when I'm not being my magnificent self. Instead of trying to fix anything, my first task is to gently ease myself back into alignment, to where relief, peace, clarity, solutions, bliss, fun, joy, exhilaration, appreciation and love abound … and then I wonder, "What on earth was I worried about again?"

CONFESSION #172 ...

WHEN I'M FEELING ALIGNED

... I love my life, I have a fabulous time no matter where I am, what I'm doing or who I'm with. Everything feels effortless, light and free. I find great pleasure in walking barefoot in the sunshine, sipping the sweetness of a liqueur coffee, sharing one with a friend, listening to the laughter of children and riding a skateboard for the first time, like I'm a kid again.

CONFESSION #173 ...

THE MOST EXHILARATING PART OF LIFE

... isn't when I get the goal, when I make the money, when I meet a new lover, when I own the next property, when I'm living the dream, the most exhilarating part is when I'm reaching for something I HOPE to have, I WANT to create, I BELIEVE I can do.

There's great value in experiencing the ups and downs of life ... they're what make the ride so worthwhile.

CONFESSION #174 ...

HOW TO HAVE THE BEST DAY EVER

HERE IS YOUR MISSION IF YOU CHOOSE TO ACCEPT IT ... Find as many excuses as you can to be happy, as many reasons as possible to feel good and as many things as you like to appreciate about yourself, your life, your mate and even your enemies ... just for a day, maybe a week, maybe even the for rest of your life ...

(This message will only self-destruct if you still aren't smiling!)

CONFESSION #175 ...

I GET REVENGE BY LOVING MY ENEMIES

Imagine the power of telling someone, "There's nothing you can say or do to stop me from knowing who you really are inside --- you're a lover, you're a magnificent creator and you're an amazing being of the finest design, whether you realise it or not!"

CONFESSION #176 ...

THE BEST WAY TO CHANGE ANYTHING

... is not to try to change others, not to try to change the conditions I see around me, not even to try to change the world

... the most fulfilling way is to change my own thoughts, beliefs, attitudes and speak more about what's already wonderful about my mate, what's already working in our world and what's already the greatest blessing in my own life

... then pretty soon the other stuff just melts into extinction!

CONFESSION #177 ...

I CAN DIFFUSE ANY CONFLICT

... by being someone who values peace over "being right", someone that cares more for taking responsibility than maintaining a position, someone who prefers to be accepting of other people's views rather than making someone else wrong. This is the characteristic of someone who values love above everything else.

CONFESSION #178 ...

SOMETIMES I FEEL REALLY BAD

... but it isn't because of something that's happened, it isn't because of my mate and it isn't because I'm not good enough! ... The only thing that ever makes me feel bad is when I have forgotten who I really am! A person who loves, a person who was born worthy, a person who uplifts others and a person who knows their heart is MUCH bigger than any problem!

CONFESSION #179 ...

LOVE MAKES MY WORLD GO ROUND

WHEN I LOVE MY FRIENDS ... I enjoy life immensely.

WHEN I LOVE MY ENEMIES ... I contribute to immense enjoyment of life on the entire planet.

CONFESSION #180 ...

I'M A LEADER

When times get tough it's not the activists who are sought, it's not the fighters who are followed, it's not the people spreading doom and gloom who are valued ... it's those who soothe the upset, it's those who share words of hope, it's those who shine a light so brightly that all the people who see it, help to illuminate the rest of the world too, and inspire leadership in all of us.

CONFESSION #181 ...

I'VE DECIDED I WON'T BE KEEPING ANY MORE SECRETS

If there's something you don't want other people to know, then don't tell me! If there's something that's so dark you are ashamed of it then don't activate it further by sharing it. Focus on things that spin your wheels, that rock your boat, that light up your life instead!

CONFESSION #182 ...

I HAVE SELECTIVE HEARING

Instead of paying attention to the statistics that gave me a higher chance of getting cancer ... I decided to "listen to my own inner being" who told me I have a good chance to live a long, healthy, happy, energized, passionate and love-filled life instead.

CONFESSION #183 …

WHAT MOST PEOPLE MIGHT CONSIDER TO BE A PITY, A PROBLEM OR A LOSS

… I consider an opportunity in disguise, a change for the best, a chance to take a new adventure, a decision to get excited about what's unfolding magnificently before me. A time to take a leap of faith into knowing that EVERYTHING I've ever asked for is on its way to me right now … and in an even more incredible form that I could ever have imagined!

CONFESSION #184 ...

I KNOW THE POWER OF UNCONDITIONAL LOVE

When I am loved unconditionally, it blows my mind … but when I love someone else without expecting anything in return, it opens my heart and connects me to soul.

CONFESSION #185 ...

I DON'T FORGIVE OTHERS BECAUSE IT'S THE RIGHT THING TO DO

I forgive others because it releases my constant need to focus on the ugliness of the past instead of noticing the incredible beauty of the future.

FORGIVENESS WOULD BE COMPLETELY UNNECESSARY

... if I refused to judge others as good or bad, saint or sinner, black or white, truthful or lying, guilty or innocent, loving or hurtful, and accepted them anyway, just as they are!

CONFESSION #186 ...

IT DOESN'T MATTER WHAT HAPPENS

... everything always works out perfectly for me, without having to get motivated, to make any extra effort or to force an outcome.

I love knowing that if I can just relax and let go of whatever I've been holding onto, most things just sort themselves out overnight ... and I've watched Toy Story! I know what goes on while I'm asleep ;-)

CONFESSION #187 ...

I'M NOT MEANT TO BE HAPPY ALL THE TIME

Sometimes I feel ease, excitement, ecstasy, and elation just for variety ;-)

CONFESSION #188 ...

EVERYTHING I NEED IS INSIDE ME

In my heart I feel the love,
In my emotions I sense the way,
In my mind I create the scene,
In my imagination I hold the vision,
In my future I see the dream,
In my soul I hold the truth,
In my source I choose to align,
In my wisdom, I know I can be and do and have anything I intend as reality for me.

CONFESSION #189 ...

I'M NOT NORMAL ... it's true!

I don't waste energy complaining about what's broken. I use it wisely to notice what's working.

I don't talk badly about myself or others. I talk about our better qualities instead.

I don't expect the worst. I imagine the best.

I don't care to listen endlessly to the problems. But I DO care to seek eternal solutions.

I don't expect you to change so I can be happy. I find happiness anyway, no matter how you are.

I don't let an issue come between me and my heart. I wait until my heart is open again and then resolve it with love.

I don't speak in haste. I choose to speak when I've taken time to find clarity first.

I don't allow people to put me down. I get out of their way until they pick themselves up.

I don't create extra drama in my life. I know I can turn on the TV and watch it there.

CONFESSION #190 ...

I APPRECIATE HOW DIFFERENT WE ARE

Life would be boring if we all had the same values, chose the same lifestyle, spoke the same language, adopted the same beliefs or followed the same rules ... for without these differences I'd have no reason to grow my heart, no purpose to expand my ideas, no need to reach for a better way to live in harmony ... and in total acceptance of your choices, whether I approve of them, understand them or would want to live that way or not!

It's diversity (not sameness) that makes us grow, that causes us to choose, that expands us into who we've now become.

CONFESSION #191 ...

ONCE UPON A TIME I LET DEPRESSION BECOME A HABIT

… of contradictory "though", negative "word", similar "action".

Then I allowed getting RELIEF to become a habit, finding benefit in each situation became a habit, focusing on happier stuff became a habit, thinking positive thoughts became a habit, moving my body more became a habit, believing in myself became a habit, appreciating what I've already got became a habit, and even loving who I am right now become a habit … then in a short amount of time, being the magnificent person I'd really always been, just became a way of life.

CONFESSION #192 …

I'M LIVING HAPPILY EVER AFTER

I once believed that two people with different dreams couldn't possibly live happily together. Then I realised that it wasn't the different dreams that were the problem, it wasn't getting a divorce that was the solution, it was just that each of them were using the other as an excuse not to keep dreaming their dream …

… but pretty soon with a little bit of practice, a dash of hope and a touch of faith, both their dreams met up and became an extraordinary combined reality, not by force, not by "working" on it, not even by setting goals … but by simply believing it might be possible, by relaxing their stringent expectations, by allowing feel-good things to dominate their conversations, by appreciating their OWN dream into life, by filling that life with love and by entrusting the "source of life" to manage ALL the finer details for them.

Living happily ever after need not be just a dream … it's the grandest adventure I've ever taken.

CONFESSION #193 ...

THE BEST WAY TO LET GO OF SOMETHING I DON'T WANT ... is to hold onto something that I do!

CONFESSION #194 ...

MY SUCCESSES ARE HUGE ... my problems are small.

The more time I take to share things that are good, the less time there is to notice the bad, although I could!
The more time I think about what's worked well in the past, the more chance I have to remember, hard times don't last!
The more times I decide to just make a new start, the more time I have to feel the peace in my heart.

CONFESSION #195 ...

THE MOST POWERFUL RELATIONSHIP STRATEGY I'VE EVER USED

... is to think, speak and write about my mate the way I want to see him, to believe that he really is the incredible guy I dream of being with, to pretend he has every good quality I could possibly want and to treat him as if he is the most wonderful man in the world ... and he just keeps proving that I'm right ;-)

It has brought us back together after a breakup, transformed our moments into sublimely passionate but most important, IT CHANGED MY ATTITUDE, it made me feel fantastic, it opened my mind and expanded my capacity to love without expecting anything in return.

CONFESSION #196 …

WHENEVER I WANT MORE MONEY

… I spend more time feeling wealthy rather than "working my butt off".

WHENEVER I WANT A RELATIONSHIP

… I take time to fall in love with life rather than "dating for the hell of it".

WHENEVER I WANT BETTER HEALTH

… I laugh and have fun as if I have a perfectly functioning body rather than "searching for a miracle cure".

WHENEVER I WANT MORE INSPIRATION

… I go and get laid ;-)

CONFESSION #197 ...

I DATED FOR THE FUN OF IT

A woman can look a certain way or just laugh and make a man turn to putty.

A man can look deeply into my eyes and make me melt.

We've all got power to draw out the best in each other. Waiting for "the right one" to come along is like NOT going to the movies until the greatest film of all time is released ... we could wait forever and miss out on all the fun.

CONFESSION #198 …

FREEDOM IS …

… choosing to be "happy" no matter what other people are doing,

… choosing to feel "love" no matter what other people are saying,

… choosing to find "peace" no matter what is going on in the world and

… choosing to "appreciate" the blessings no matter what circumstance confronts me.

CONFESSION #199 ...

I ADORE THE SIMPLE THINGS IN LIFE

I just love it when it gets cold enough to light the wood fire, to have extra reason to snuggle closer to my man, to appreciate the gentle warmth filtering through a cup of continental drinking chocolate, to throw on a coat I've been waiting all summer to wear! The feeling I get when I stop and take the time to appreciate something, gives me as much pleasure as life itself.

CONFESSION #200 ...

I HAVE ACCESS TO INFINITE INTELLIGENCE

… and it doesn't require waiting for a burning bush, lightning to strike, writings in stone or evaluating words written thousands of years ago. We're all receiving guidance every minute of the day ... it's innate and it's natural. It hasn't been given to some and not others; it doesn't need supernatural occurrences or even deep meditation.

If it feels GOOD it's guidance, if it feels BAD it's also guidance.

CONFESSION #201 ...

I FOLLOW MY PASSIONS

... which sometimes involves outrageous risk, the ridicule of friends, seemingly crazy choices and giving up doing what society considers "the norm".

But without risk there would be no exhilaration, no intense passion and no deep desire to reach for something that heightens my sense of aliveness ... and when I feel alive, I have clearer access to my connection with God, and then the risk just becomes one great adventure.

CONFESSION #202 ...

I'M ENJOYING THE RIDE OF MY LIFE

Sometimes it's predictable. I like that. Sometimes it takes me by surprise. I like that too. Most of the time it just flows on with its ups and downs and I adapt, I make it work for me and accept it as part of the excitement. There will always be another bridge to cross, another road to travel, a reason to expand my mind and open my heart wider than it was before. Every contrasting experience causes me to grow, to write better, to re-define who I am.

No matter what happens - it's all good!

CONFESSION #203 ...

I'VE FOUND REAL LOVE .... that can never be taken away, than can never hurt, that can never fade.

Love is often stimulated by another person, by a pet, by nature, by art or by certain activities etc, but they are just the catalyst that calls the love that IS us, through us.

What I've found now is a resonance with my own source, a connection to my soul, a feeling of oneness with all that is, and with that profound power, I can focus on almost anything and "love it" into life.

CONFESSION #204 ...

I'M THERE FOR YOU EVEN WHEN YOU THINK I'M NOT

... but I've taught myself to concentrate on your solution, not listen to your problem. I've faced myself in the direction of your answer, not on the dilemma of your question. I've focused my imagination on your incredible wellness not on the pain of your illness ... and the strength of my vision will bring you closer to knowing it too.

CONFESSION #205 ...

I TAKE TIME OUT TO NURTURE MYSELF

By nature a feminine woman is a "giver", a "lover" and a "nurturer".

When she starts to feel a little overwhelmed (or resentful) with all she has done for her family, friends, her kids, her business or her mate, it is a sign she needs to take time out and nurture her own soul so she can once again FEEL the essence of "who she really is", to more joyously GIVE all that she has to give and to profoundly BE who she was made to be.

CONFESSION #206 …

SOMETIMES A PROBLEM IS NOT WHAT IT SEEMS TO BE

A wise man once told me, that when I think my problem is related to my relationship, it is most often related to finances instead. If I think my problem is related to money, it is most likely my relationship that needs attention. And if I have no problems to overcome, I really need to create some and stir things up a bit … lol

CONFESSION #207 ...

I CAN SEE BENEATH YOUR PAIN

Your thoughts could draw out my thunder, but all I feel is calmness through the eye of the storm.
Your words are tempting, but all I hear is your heart beating.
Your behaviour shows confusion, but all I see is the clarity in your eyes.
Your soul cries out for forgiveness and my tears of appreciation for the life we share together wash away the pain and uncover the deepest love.

CONFESSION #208 ...

I CAN'T REALLY CHANGE YOUR OPINION OF ME

... all I can do is be so convinced, so sure and so knowing of "who I really am" that it makes me even more determined to live my own life with integrity.

CONFESSION #209 …

IT'S ALL GETTING CLOSER

The love I enjoy feeling is only a heartbeat away.

Relief from stress is only a deep breath away.

Getting back on track is only a new thought away.

Resolving an issue is only a "changed attitude" away.

Moving closer to others is only an outstretched hand away.

A more prosperous bank balance is only a belief away.

Happiness is only a choice away!

CONFESSION #210 ...

WHEN I WANT TO FEEL BETTER THAN I DO

... and when all else fails, "making peace" with where I am is the perfect place to start.

It provides a sense of relief, it lets me know I don't have to fix this right now, it enables the solutions to come in much more creative ways than I could have imagined and it helps me relax and remember that tranquility, harmony and love are dominant vibrations in my world.

CONFESSION #211 ...

I'M GREEDY ... for the good things in life. For those, I spend endless hours gorging myself.

CONFESSION #212 ...

I DON'T NEED YOU TO LOVE ME

… as much as you are loving who you are becoming. I don't require others to follow, I'd rather they follow their heart, their dreams, their passion. I don't need fans, I prefer that you fan the flames of desire now burning inside and I don't want to be worshiped, I encourage you to stand in awe of your precious uniqueness and align in wholeness with your own blessed soul.

CONFESSION #213 ...

I'M NEVER ALONE

I AM WHERE I AM and it's the perfect place to start.

I HAVE what I have, and it's more than enough.

I AM CREATING what I'm creating by what I think, say and do.

I AM GOING where I'm going and a thousand angels are with me too.

CONFESSION #214 …

I'M GLAD I FEEL PAIN

… for without it I'd never know when I'm using my thoughts, my words or my actions in ways that take me "closer to" or "further from" where I want to go. If I simply change what I am thinking, saying or doing I can find relief in an instant.

Prolonging the pain by giving it further attention is optional … Suffering is self-inflicted.

When you focus on pain, you notice the pain, and make it bigger, so big that you can't feel anything else. When you focus on something that makes you smile, you notice more of what makes you smile, and make it bigger, so big that you really can't see anything else. When you focus on something you love, you notice even more love, and you make it bigger, so big that you just can't imagine that there was ever anything else.

CONFESSION #215 ...

I PRAY OFTEN, NOT JUST WHEN I'M IN TROUBLE

... and the most heart-warming prayers are those of appreciation for where I've come from, what I already have and what I'm about to receive. But even in my darkest hours, I've always received help and sometimes in the most amazing ways ...

When I have felt doubt, I ask to find hope.
When I have felt hate, I ask to uncover the grandest love.
When I have felt hurt, I ask to know the stillness of peace.
When I have felt resentment, I ask to seek forgiveness of self.
When I have felt troubled, I ask to sense the deepest calm.
When I have felt judgment, I ask to cultivate greater understanding.
When I have felt stressed, I ask to take a deep breath of relief.
When I have felt like a failure, I ask to know my inevitable success.
When I have felt annoyance, I ask to remember to have patience and trust.
When I have felt separation, I ask to reunite with my inner being who is always here for me.
When I have felt in bondage, I ask to give myself the freedom to feel the fullness of my own blessed soul.

CONFESSION #216 ...

I ONLY DO WHAT I WANT TO DO

Each day I make two lists.

1. What I intend to do today.
2. What I am giving to the universe/God to manage for me.

Wisdom is, knowing what I can control, letting go what I don't want to do and being willing to admit the truth about it. The universe has NEVER failed to deliver whatever I have asked for in the moment I've released the resistance to receiving it!

CONFESSION #217 ...

I DON'T EVEN BUY PRESENTS

I only give people what I'm inspired to give!
I don't give more to someone in distress and less to those who are strong.
I don't give out of obligation or with expectation of getting anything in return.

When I released the incessant need to follow society's habit of gifts at Christmas and eggs at Easter, I found I had so much more of ME to give, and that's the greatest gift of all.

CONFESSION #218 ...

I'M HEALTHY, WEALTHY AND HAPPY

If wealth was measured in happiness ... I'll be one of the richest people in the world.
If health was measured by a positive outlook ... I'll keep on feeling fabulous until the day I die.
If happiness was measured by the smile on my face, the warmth in my heart and the peace in my soul ... I'll be in joy, ecstasy and bliss forever.

Now that's heaven on earth!

CONFESSION #219 ...

I LOVE ASKING FOR HELP AND MOST MEN LOVE GIVING IT

They feel useful when they have something to do, they feel happy when I appreciate the simple things, and they feel proud about being able to fix stuff that I'd rather not. They thrive on having a job, a plan, a purpose. A masculine man needs a mission as much as the air that he breathes.

CONFESSION #220 ...

EVERYTHING IS ALL ABOUT ME

When I think it's about someone else – it's about me.

When I decide someone isn't giving me what I need – it's about me.

When I judge someone else as wrong – it's really me.

Whenever I think someone else should change so I can feel better, I look in the mirror first and make sure my relationship with me is reflecting on the outside, the person I really am on the inside.

CONFESSION #221 ...

I FIND MY OWN EMPOWERMENT

The only time I ever feel DIS-EMPOWERED is when I'm expecting someone else ...

... to make me happy
... to love me
... to provide stability
... to approve
... to be proud of me
... to entertain
... to help me grow
... to make me feel like I matter
... to fulfill my soul purpose

To feel EMPOWERED, I give these things to myself first and then fill up so full, that the overflow naturally showers others.

CONFESSION #222 ...

I LOVE FACEBOOK

It's been the catalyst for enormous fun, initiating some wonderful relationships, distracting me from my worries, gaining loads of inspiration, getting laid, growing incredibly through the contrast of my own and other peoples experiences, making the most delightful connections, writing some amazing books, being given a publishing contract, making an abundance of money and getting more fabulous clients than any other single source has ever done.

On Facebook I am ME, just larger than life!

CONFESSION #223 ...

LOVE MAKES LIFE WORTHWHILE

Loving my friends is easy, accepting the people I approve of is easy, understanding those who have similar values is easy ... but the greatest gift I ever give myself is when I open my heart to my enemies, when I accept those who make different choices, when I decide I no longer need to control the people I just don't understand and choose to love the person I know inside they really are anyway!

CONFESSION #224 ...

WHEN I FLOW LOVE

... time disappears, differences become irrelevant, emotions flow freely, moods are elevated, hate is dissolved, wrongs are forgiven, wounds are healed, trouble turns to calm, doubt transforms into hope, physical distance is bridged, judgment is replaced with understanding, stress is released, agitation changes to patience, pain turns into relief, beliefs that held me captive are replaced with a sense of freedom, what was once viewed as failure can now be seen as real success, petty annoyances become laughable, my body finally relaxes, the mind is quietened, my heart expands and my soul unites with the energy of the source of life that draws forth a feeling of indescribable oneness with "all that is".

CONFESSION #225 ...

I LOVE LOVING

I love the rain and the sunshine, the magnificent view, my wonderful guy, the funny little dog, the clean fresh air, delicious home cooked food, the sound of gently blowing wind chimes ... I use anything as an excuse to love, because that always brings me closer to feeling the blissful essence of all that I am.

When I am feeling my most loving self I more naturally see the best in the people around me, find many things to appreciate and thank them for and it gives them the space and desire to care for me, make plans to spend time with me and serve my needs too ... and they do it by choice, not out of obligation.

CONFESSION #226 …

I LOVE BEING VALUED BY MY MAN

… to allow him to enjoy the curves of my body, to share with him the warmth from my heart, to have him draw insight from my mind and to develop an even more precious bond, as we align our souls with the divine.

I LOVE TO TALK ABOUT HOW MUCH MY MAN MEANS TO ME

… to think about the special things he does, to remember all the fun we've had, to imagine an even happier future and to catch him doing things I like and tell him how much I appreciate them.

I feel like I'm being the best I can be when I give more energy to the positive aspects and let the negative ones disappear gently into oblivion.

CONFESSION #227 ...

I HAVE GREAT FAITH ... and often choose to believe blindly in something I can't see evidence of YET.

Having faith in something life enhancing transforms lives, defies reality, re-establishes wellness, harmonises relationships, renews a vision for the future and revitalizes my energy for living ... But I can only instill faith in my heart when my mind stops needing proof that something is already true.

CONFESSION #228 ...

WHILE MOST PEOPLE WANT TO BE WITH SOMEONE WHO LOVES "THEM"

... I like to be with a person who loves themselves.

CONFESSION #229 ...

I ENJOY WHAT I HAVE IN EACH MOMENT

... and don't have an expectation that it will last forever, that it will always give me what I need, that it will even be there for me to remember. Life is good now ... and I peacefully let go that which no longer wishes to remain and allow new and even better things to flow ever so gently into my evolving experience of life.

CONFESSION #230 ...

I HAVE NO REGRETS

... and if YOU also knew what was on its way to you right now, you would not use one moment shedding a tear of regret, one instant thinking about what you would have done different, one minute worrying about what you've lost ... you would only think about what there was to gain, only remember how much you have grown and only look with excited anticipation towards what is about to be the next great adventure of your entire life.

The next great adventure is NOT something we even need to think about .... the next great adventure is always inspired from the heart, it is born from the contrast we have lived, it is moulded out of all our secret desires, our wishes and passions and it flows to us swiftly, sweeps us away gently and holds us in its loving embrace from now unto eternity ... as soon as we relax, in the very moment we allow it and in the instant we decide to say "YES", I knew you were here waiting for me all along.

CONFESSION #231 ...

THE WORLD IS MY PLAYGROUND

Everywhere I go people treat me well. Everything I do is because I want to, because it feels right, because I'm inspired, because it brings me joy, because who I am inside is someone who loves to live, someone who loves to love, someone who loves to give of myself and someone who loves to feel good. And when I feel like this, life always unfolds in the most delightful ways.

CONFESSION #232 ...

MY LIFE IS CONSTANTLY TRANSFORMING

… like the metamorphosis of a tiny caterpillar into a majestic butterfly. I often imagine I'm on the brink of experiencing more peace, more love, more joy, more bliss, more ecstasy and more abundance than ever before. Things just keep on getting better and better for me.

In each moment I have an opportunity, to face towards what's causing me discomfort or towards what I prefer to create instead ... and then keenly focus my attention on that new direction, never to look back, unless in deep appreciation for what the past experience has joyously caused me to create.

CONFESSION #233 ...

LIFE IS SUCH A GREAT GAME TO PLAY

The more I practice going to bed being thankful for what I've already been given and waking up with appreciation for what I'm about to receive, the higher my emotional states become ... and even in heightened states, there is contrast. Before I may have experienced anything from fear or powerlessness to happiness, these days I float between the occasional doubt to mostly ecstasy, joy and bliss.

I keep playing with life to make it become what it is.

CONFESSION #234 ...

I HAVE THE POWER

The power to choose where I place my attention.

The power to decide which conversations I'll engage in.

The power to take time out when I need it.

The power to stop expecting myself and others to behave so perfectly.

The power to think more positive thoughts, speak more supportive words and to give unconditionally from my heart because it is who I intend to be.

CONFESSION #235 ...

I KNOW WHEN TO LET GO

… of all the things I can't control, which is everything except my thoughts, my words and my actions.

There's a time to possess and a time to set free,
a time to imitate and a time to be me,
a time to plant and a time to sow,
a time stay and a time to go.

I take responsibility for what is mine and leave the rest in the loving hands of the divine.

CONFESSION #236 ...

WHEN I'M FEELING DOWN

I start by making peace with where I'm at.
I accept that I'm experiencing a moment of contrast and that it will pass by soon.
I get relief in the best way I can.
I remind myself that "things have always worked out before" and trust that I'm on the brink of something so wonderful, that my decision to step back from trying to control it, will allow the miracles to occur even quicker.

CONFESSION #237 ...

I LOVE AND ACCEPT MYSELF, JUST THE WAY I AM.

I LOVE AND ACCEPT MY EMOTIONAL PROCESS, JUST THE WAY IT IS TOO.

If I've been in despair, expressing rage can help me feel a little bit better.
If I've felt powerless, getting really angry or getting revenge is a way to help me feel a little bit better.
When I am in the throes of anger, instead of feeling guilty (and making myself feel bad again), I blame someone else for a while, which helps me feel a little bit better.
When I've been blaming someone else for long enough, letting myself feel disappointed is a couple steps up the emotional scale too.
When I've been feeling disappointed, overwhelmed or even bored, just finding thoughts of hope is the start of feeling so much more positive again.

When I allow myself to "feel" my underlying emotions and express them, I flow so much more easily back to my naturally unconditionally loving nature ... just like I did when I was a child!

CONFESSION #238 …

I LOVE MYSELF SO MUCH

… that I won't speak badly about someone else simply because it makes me feel bad. I refuse to see them in a negative light because it takes my emotions into a deathly downward dive. We often think the problem with relationships is that one doesn't love the other enough … I think it's that the individual is NOT paying enough attention to loving themselves.

I LOVE MYSELF SO MUCH that I get over what someone else is doing with their lives and get on with being a good example with mine.

I LOVE MYSELF SO MUCH that I won't allow myself to feel worse by focusing on what someone else is doing when they're disconnected from who they really are.

… I can't change what they've done in the past by talking about it,
… I can't change what they're doing now by making it wrong and
… and I certainly can't change what they're about to do in the future by condemning them.

I LOVE MYSELF SO MUCH that I only speak well of myself and others. In the moment I tell someone something negative … I am projecting separation through a judgment from my mind. In the moment I tell someone something positive, I am reflecting wholeness and the wisdom of the divine.

CONFESSION #239 ...

WHEN I BRING ATTENTION TO SOMEONE ELSE'S WEAKNESS

... it deflates both of us.

WHEN I TRAIN MYSELF TO FOCUS ONLY ON OUR STRENGTHS

... it elevates the consciousness of all.

CONFESSION #240 ...

THE MOST LIBERATING DECISIONS I EVER MADE

STOP caring about what other people might think of me.
STOP comparing myself to others.
STOP trying to fix what I think is wrong with the world ...

... and then START to do what feels right to ME, what makes ME feel better and what lights up my universe!

CONFESSION #241 ...

I DON'T DO DRUGS

... but, when I'm feeling the fullness of my higher self I do ecstasy, joy, exhilaration and bliss with ease and grace.

CONFESSION #242 …

I DON'T TALK ABOUT MY PROBLEMS

… I prefer entertainment that lifts people up.

CONFESSION #243 …

I DON'T NEED TO TRAVEL

… my whole life is a holiday!

CONFESSION #244 ...

I DON'T TRY TO FIX ANYONE

... instead I build them up by appreciating their positive aspects, acknowledging their strengths and finding out what makes them come alive, what lights up their world and enhance everyone's experience of life even more!

Appreciation is a powerful influencer. Can you remember how good it feels to be around uplifting people? They naturally draw out the special parts of our personality and it makes us shine.

CONFESSION #245 ...

GETTING MORE STUFF DOESN'T MAKE ME HAPPY FOR LONG

... but when I take the time to appreciate what someone else has done, when I stop for a moment and imagine who they really are, when I relax for an instant and remember the amazing blessings I've already been given, I'm filled with endless joy beyond description. That's where happiness really starts ... on the inside!

CONFESSION #246 ...

I CAN ALWAYS FEEL BETTER

No matter what's happened,

I can remember something from the past that makes me feel better, I can do something in the present that makes me feel better and I can imagine something amazing for my future that lures me into its web of creative reality.

REALITY IS ... Whatever I imagine it to be!

CONFESSION #247 ...

I GO NAKED AS OFTEN AS I CAN

I've always considered the body to be a beautiful thing, to be shown with pride not to be hidden in disgust, to be cherished with care, to be lavished with attention, to be adored with all its "perceived" imperfections, to be celebrated in all its glory. The freer I am with my body, the freer I feel in my mind and the freer I am to connect more intimately with my soul!

CONFESSION #248 ...

GOOD THINGS KEEP HAPPENING

... no matter where I'm at, no matter what it might seem like, no matter how negative I might be. It's just a lot easier to see the good things coming when I'm looking forward towards a brighter future, rather than looking back at my darkest past.

CONFESSION #249 …

I HAVE MONEY COMING OUT MY EARS … I think it's a good look … don't you?

CONFESSION #250 ...

I HOPE I NEVER GET SERIOUS

Serious never accomplished anything worthwhile, but I do love to get HAPPY! Happy with who I've become, happy with what I've achieved, happy with the life I have already lived, happy about the next adventure I'm gonna take, happy with all the new friends I'm still to make.

CONFESSION #251 ...

I'M SO EXCITED TODAY

I'm sure it's a sin, it should be illegal, I must be on drugs, the realists can't understand, someone should lock me up, perhaps I'm insane, I'm definitely not normal, it keeps getting worse, it can't be contained ... it's spreading like a disease ... watch out, you might catch it! ... :-)

CONFESSION #252 ...

I LIKE TO BRING OUT THE BEST IN EVERYONE

I don't want you to walk away just thinking I'm wonderful, I want you to walk away resonating deeply with your own version of magnificence.

CONFESSION #253 ...

MY SECRET TO SUCCESSFUL RELATIONSHIPS

… has little to do with my mate and everything to do with my attitude about him. When I amplify the happy times from the PAST, when I notice what is working in the PRESENT while keeping an eye focused on what I want to create in the FUTURE, my relationships thrive.

Without VISION relationships perish!

CONFESSION #254 ...

THE MOST IMPORTANT RELATIONSHIP ... is the one I have with myself.

When I am aligned with my own dreams and desires, I can do nothing but flourish.

When other people align with their OWN dreams and desires, we all flourish together.

Relationship energy dissipates when we both try to align with each other.

Relationship energy is expanded the moment one or both of us chooses to align with our maker.

CONFESSION #255 ...

THE POSSIBILITIES ARE ENDLESS

WOMEN seem to be more excited by the "possibility" of love than by actually receiving it. That's why anticipating the arrival of the man of our dreams is so deliciously intoxicating.

A WOMAN can have the man of her dreams and still be unhappy. If she uses her mind to remember all the romantic things he did in the past, acknowledge the wonderful things he's doing in the present and dream of the romantic things he could do for her in the future, she will rediscover the magic of love pulsating in her own heart again ... Dream big!

MEN seem to be more excited by the "possibility" of success rather than by actually achieving it. That's why when they reach a goal, they feel the immediate need to set up a new challenge.

A MAN can have position, power and prestige and still feel dissatisfied with his lot. When he uses his mind to think about the amazing things he's achieved in the past, praise himself for what he's doing well in the present and set up a new game to play in the future, he reignites the passion for challenge burning deep in his soul ... Enjoy the journey!

CONFESSION #256 ...

MY LIFE CHANGED INSTANTLY WITH ONE SIMPLE DECISION

I decided that being happy was the most important thing to me!

If something doesn't feel good I pay it no attention. If something does feel good I give it all the time in the world.

In the moment that decision was made, it aligned me fully with my dreams, with my love of adventure, with my passion for living and with the source of life eternal ... and it sorted out the sheep from the goats ;-)

CONFESSION #257 ...

GOD DOESN'T HAVE A PLAN FOR MY LIFE

I set my own plan in motion the very moment I wished for something to be better. God just remembers it all and guides me endlessly towards it.

When I relax I move closer, when I trust I move closer, when I have faith I move closer, when I realise that what I've asked for has already been given, I am there, living my own incredible dream.

CONFESSION #258 ...

I APPRECIATE CHALLENGE AS MUCH AS COMFORT

An "easy ride" enables me to float gently along with the current.

A "rough ride" carves out an even wider version of the stream - one that can manage any torrential downpour and expand my capacity to pursue the most exhilarating ride of my life.

CONFESSION #259 ...

MY PAST IS IRRELEVANT

This precious moment provides the greatest opportunity to move towards the future I have always dreamed myself having.

CONFESSION #260 …

MY CURRENT REALITY IS IRRELEVANT

… this moment just passed, this moment just passed, this moment just passed!

When I'm driving on the road, I don't look down to where the wheels are turning, I don't look back at where I've been and I don't even try to see around the corners, I just look ahead as much as I need towards my destination, and the vehicle of life takes me to where I really intended to go all along.

CONFESSION #261 ...

I CAN'T MOVE ON TO A BETTER RELATIONSHIP

... until I've first changed my thoughts, my story, my beliefs, my attitude and my vibration about the last.

CONFESSION #262 ...

THE BEST THING I EVER DID FOR MY RELATIONSHIP

... was to stop trying to improve my mate.

When I genuinely gave up needing him to be different, he started to transform in front of my eyes, physically, mentally, supportively and soulfully. Together we are finding tremendous value in overcoming conflict and I for one look forward to creating some occasionally, just for fun.

CONFESSION #263 …

THE BEST THING MY MAN EVER DID FOR OUR RELATIONSHIP

… was to stop trying to fix me whenever I felt a bit "off".

When he gave up expecting me to be calm, loving and always able to meet his needs, and just relaxed and let me be how I was instead … he stopped turning me into the bitch from hell and awakened the goddess of his dreams.

CONFESSION #264 ...

MY RELATIONSHIP BROKE UP

... now we're getting on better than when we first met! But, it isn't a commitment to each other that keeps us together ... it's allowing the other to have their own dreams, to find their own purpose, to follow their own passions, to decide their own path and to fulfill their own needs, that creates peace, encourages harmony, expands happiness and brings two "whole" individuals closer than ever before.

CONFESSION #265 ...

LOVE SOLVES ALL OUR RELATIONSHIP CHALLENGES

WHEN A WOMAN GETS ANGRY ... and a man is in his heart ... he finds her feminine fury really sexy. It's impossible for a woman to stay angry with a horny man who looks her lovingly in the eyes no matter what crazy things come out her mouth.

WHEN A MAN GETS CONFUSED ... and a woman is in her heart ... she accepts that a man is gonna stuff up occasionally, has faith that he'll work things out himself and remembers that he hardly ever understands what she's talking about no matter how much he tries. But it's virtually impossible for a man to be confused about a womans intentions, when she trusts him completely no matter what.

(It only takes ONE OF US to be in our hearts for this to work perfectly ... I promise you! See confession #270)

CONFESSION #266 ...

MY RELATIONSHIP HAS A GREATER PURPOSE

My man knows that I have the ability, will and desire to love unconditionally. He knows that I don't need an excuse to love, that loving is what comes naturally to me. The greatest gift he can give me is stir things up a bit so that I get extra opportunities to love unconditionally – which is by far, the greatest experience of all!

CONFESSION #267 ...

I LOVE YOU

... not because I expect something in return, but because it is an expression of who I really am.

CONFESSION #268 ...

I LOVE BEING IN A RELATIONSHIP

My man was first attracted to me physically and I was attracted to him because I felt safe to express my emotions in his presence. Now he has progressed all the way to highly valuing his own emotional expression and knowing he'll be loved anyway. I have progressed to highly valuing the physical connection, knowing I can be naked and vulnerable and know that he will protect, cherish and adore me even more.

CONFESSION #269 ...

COMMITTING TO A RELATIONSHIP REALLY WORKS

... but I didn't commit to the relationship with my mate, I made a commitment to my relationship with ME first!

When I began to love and accept myself just the way I am, I found I could love and accept my emotional process just the way it is too ... It was then I understood what everyone else was wanting as well ... to be loved and accepted WITHOUT someone trying to fix us, change us, counsel us, coach us, instruct us, discipline us or even sympathize with us.

Change occurs naturally, in the moment I stop trying to MAKE something better happen in my relationship and begin to relax and simply ALLOW it to transform.

CONFESSION #270 ...

IT ONLY TAKES ONE OF US

… to stop adding fuel to an argument, to diffuse a problem with understanding, to bring a relationship closer by loving unconditionally, to trust someone to find their own answers and empower their independence. When I stopped saying, "if only other people felt like this too" I empowered myself to make the change inside me, that I wanted to see outside in the world.

CONFESSION #271 ...

I DON'T JUST HANG AROUND LIKE-MINDED PEOPLE

I hang around people who are totally different to me too, and find they are the ones who give me the most opportunity to expand to a higher level, to open my mind wider, to embrace our uniqueness and love unconditionally no matter how different we are. I don't do it because I feel sorry for them, because I think they deserve it or because I think I should ... I do it because I am worth it.

CONFESSION #272 ...

WHEN A RELATIONSHIP IS MAKING ME FEEL UNCOMFORTABLE

... I change my attitude about it before I change anything else!

I consciously choose to change how I feel by focusing on things that make me feel good right now and by dreaming the most exciting dreams for my future. My mate/friend is either attracted back strongly into my sphere of influence or floats away on the very next breeze, seamlessly allowing someone who is a perfect vibrational match to me, to enter instead.

I never have reason to take a permanent trip away from anyone ... but I often find reason to choose a new attitude that enlivens all of us.

CONFESSION #273 ...

I CAN FEEL HOW EASY IT IS

... to bask in the beauty of nature ... to enjoy the sounds of the birds chirping ... to soak up the morning sunshine... to smell the deliciousness of coffee brewing ... to think about my lover and know the warmth of his touch ... to imagine the most magnificent future for all of us. I've decided to take a new emotional journey now! How about you?

CONFESSION #274 …

I LOVE BEING STIMULATED

… by heart pumping interactions, emotionally freeing expressions, mentally stimulating discussions, the most erotic physical intimacy and deep soulful connections. I don't have a preference for just one, I love them all.

CONFESSION #275 ...

I SHARE WHAT I AM LEARNING

I use words to instruct, I use metaphors as examples, I use descriptions to stimulate imagination, I use suggestions to open the mind, I ask questions to make you think, I use positivity to soothe the emotions, I use faith to uplift your spirits ... but demonstration is by far the most powerful way to share anything. I'm thoughtful about what I share with the world each day!

CONFESSION #276 ...

I HAVE NO RULES FOR ME, I HAVE NO RULES FOR YOU

… I prefer to take each precious moment to decide what I will do. And feel the freedom that's known when, "to myself I am true!"

CONFESSION #277 ...

I MAKE THINGS COME TRUE ... with everything I think, say and do.

I enjoy choosing the pathway of thought I will pursue, the memories to hold, the words that I use, the beliefs I decide, the body posture I assume, the conversations to have and the actions I do ... and know that the power is in my hands to feel good or bad, turned on or off, living with passion or dying of despair.

I choose to live a life beyond compare!

CONFESSION #278 …

I LOVE OTHER PEOPLE SO EASILY

… by having the self-discipline to focus only on the best parts of them, to see them as the source of all life sees them, to believe they have already found their solution, to know they have already achieved their wellness, to imagine them as perfectly whole, to envision them as already being the person I know they really are, inside their heart of hearts.

CONFESSION #279 ...

MY MAN AND I HAVE STARTED A FIGHT

… over who loves each other the most. The competition is on!

CONFESSION #280 ...

IT DOESN'T MATTER

It doesn't matter what I love, when I love, why I love or how I love ... it's allowing love to flow through me that's the source of my greatest energy, strength, pleasure, joy, abundance, foresight, clarity and bliss.

CONFESSION #281 ...

I DON'T PLAN ... I DREAM!

I don't strive ... I allow.
I don't stress ... I relax.
I don't live within my means,
I live as if I can have anything I desire
and the ways and the means are timely inspired.
I leave the management to God
and just get on with my job.
Then, when I look back at what I had asked for before,
I notice the many blessings that already walked through my door.

CONFESSION #282 …

I MADE MY MAN FALL IN LOVE WITH ME

… he didn't have a chance!

Love doesn't criticize, love doesn't notice the bad, love doesn't focus on what's wrong, love appreciates everything it has ever had! Love doesn't require something in return, love doesn't ever need to be concerned, love just gives without any need … expressing itself openly in thought, word and deed.

CONFESSION #283 ...

I ACCEPT IT WHEN SOMEONE DROPS OUT OF MY LIFE

... but if it was me who made the decision to leave, I can experience all sorts of trauma.

I realised that closing my heart hurts me more than anything anyone else can ever do, and the more time I spend justifying WHY it should have ended, the deeper entrenched in the issue I become. Now I allow people to come and go as they please and just concentrate on being the best ME I can be.

CONFESSION #284 …

IN THE PAST WHEN I CLOSED MY HEART

… I had accidents, hurt myself, felt irrationally depressed, became ill, got sucked into silly arguments, fell into unforeseen circumstances and attracted all manner of unpleasant experiences. Yet for all those experiences I am eternally appreciative, as they showed me clearly that I was "off track".

Now if I feel discomfort in any form, I ask, who have I stopped loving? Sometimes the answer is "ME".

In the moment that I opened my heart again, the weight lifted, I miraculously cured myself, I was inspired to the next action, I knew instinctively who I was again and I remembered who you are too … we are all lovers, of divine design, just expressing it in a myriad of different ways.

I LOVE AND ACCEPT ALL OF US

I don't choose to love and accept other people because it will help them, I choose to love and accept them because it reconnects me to the open, warm-hearted, understanding and whole person I know inside I really am.

CONFESSION #285 ...

I LEARNED HOW TO LOVE UNCONDITIONALLY

I found it hard to believe that someone could love me like I wanted to be loved ... but it wasn't until I practiced "being" the love I wanted to receive, that I understood its real power.

When I expect nothing in return for the love I offer it's impossible to be hurt, it's impossible to doubt, it's impossible to feel insecure and it's impossible to go back to loving conditionally ever again. I don't need proof that it works. I don't care if you believe me and it doesn't matter if you love me or not! Flowing love through me is the most intoxicating, joy-filled freedom of all.

I love you, and you, and you, and you ... no exceptions :-)

The clearest form of unconditional love comes from MYSELF, to myself, for myself, then shared with others ... yet it can sometimes come from another, because of another, in spite of another but mostly because it's just who I am!

CONFESSION #286 ...

LOVE FEELS BETTER THAN ANY OTHER EMOTION

I uncovered an even more expanded definition of love by saying "yes" to relationships, just like I discovered my own experience of God by saying "yes" to life. To me they are one and the same. Love and life are the most satisfying games of all.

CONFESSION #287 ...

I'VE FOUND LOVE IN ALL SORTS OF PLACES

... in the silence of my heart and through the words from my lips, in the stillness of the moment and the fury of intense passion. I've felt it in sorrow as well as in great joy and known its beauty in death and in a baby's first breath. There's nowhere that love cannot be found, for even fear is born from love ... the love of life itself.

CONFESSION #288 …

I AM LOVING MENOPAUSE

Menopause is a powerful phase of a woman's cycle when our hormones adapt from being productive to being stable. Some decide it is a "bad thing" and choose to believe negative reports, tell others their sad tales and spread rumours of impending doom. For me, I choose it to be a time of freedom, relaxation, nurturing, expanded wisdom and increased emotional mastery.

CONFESSION #289 ...

WHEN I DECLARE SOMETHING PUBLICLY

... I make it more real than when I just think about it. When I have faith that something will become true, it comes true in even better ways than if I had tried to make it happen. When I focus on what makes me feel really good, I feel really good and attract other good things into my reality. Life is always a reflection of the way I believe, feel, choose, declare and intend it to be!

CONFESSION #290 ...

I AM AN ETERNAL OPTIMIST

I believe that one person who is continuously negative can drown readily in a sea of strife, and one person who is forever inspiring can lead millions to the fountain of life.

CONFESSION #291 ...

I MAKE FUN OF MY PROBLEMS ... and sometimes I'll make fun of yours too.

The more I take life lightly, the more I find reason to laugh, the more I concentrate on the things that make me feel better, the more I focus on what is already working out for me ... the quicker it's all resolved.

CONFESSION #292 ...

I WONDERED IF I HAD ANYTHING OF VALUE TO CONTRIBUTE TO THE WORLD

Then I decided to remember all the times I'd made someone laugh, I reached out my hand, I accepted another, I said a comforting word, I paid a compliment, I helped someone feel useful again, I cooked a great meal, I got up in the middle of the night to comfort a crying child, I smiled at a stranger, I let go a past hurt, I forgave an old friend, I made peace with an enemy ... and it was then that I realized, just how much I'd already done.

CONFESSION #293 ...

I DON'T POINT OUT OTHER PEOPLES WEAKNESSES

We all know when we haven't been our naturally loving selves because we feel really bad, and having someone point it out to us just makes us feel worse ... but being around people who remind us how incredible we normally are, helps us get back to our preferred self so much quicker.

CONFESSION #294 ...

I'M ON A PERMANENT "VERBAL" FAST

I only speak if I have something useful to share. The profound love and gentle peace that's contained in silence, is pure bliss.

CONFESSION #295 ...

I'VE DECIDED TO LET OTHER PEOPLE LOVE ME ... I just can't fight it any more ;-)

CONFESSION #296 ...

WHEN I LET OTHER PEOPLE LOVE ME

I STOP doing and START being ... being someone who is deserving, being someone who was born worthy, being someone who can be vulnerable, being someone who allows others the intense pleasure, pure power and loving release that comes from giving without needing anything in return.

LIVING fully involves taking risks. LOVING fully involves letting go of control.

CONFESSION #297 ...

IT'S ALWAYS MY CHOICE

I can talk about how someone has hurt me ... OR I can choose to recall all the times they cared for me.

I can notice the ways that someone is avoiding me ... OR I can choose to remember all the times they attended to my needs.

I can think about how I'm not being loved in the way I want to be loved ... OR I can choose to focus on the times I loved myself so much that it was irrelevant whether they did or not.

It's always my choice, to concentrate on what's just happened OR on what I really want. Either way, I get more of whatever I'm giving my attention to so NOW I'm gonna think so much more about that!

CONFESSION #298 ...

WHEN I THINK SOMEONE ELSE IS REALLY TO BLAME

… it's always my attitude that's in need of a change.
So I dust myself off and decide to play a new game.

STOP focusing on the negatives … build from the positives.
STOP talking about their shortcomings … remember their magnificence.
STOP thinking that "they" are the problem … know that "I" am the solution.
STOP reacting to their smallness … demonstrate my greatness.
STOP concentrating on the bad times … remind them of the good ones.
STOP withholding what they're wanting … give it unconditionally.
STOP expecting the worst … imagine the best.
STOP wanting them to change … change my own attitude.
STOP fighting for my rights … find peace in my heart and be the person I have always known I truly am.

CONFESSION #299 ...

I DESERVE THE BEST

… and when I see the best, feel the best, remember the best, imagine the best and forget about the rest, I experience the incredible power I have to create my own magnificent life, with all the glorious magic that it's meant to contain. The best is most definitely yet to come.

CONFESSION #300 …

THE BEST PART OF LIFE IS YET TO COME …

When I'm enchanted by the future and not obsessed with the past, life takes on new meaning where no dark shadows can be cast. There's not one thing I can dream of that cannot be given, by this abundant universe … vibrationally driven.

When I feel positive emotion, all good things are drawn, towards me with haste, soon after the thought has been born. To live life with forward vision of what's possible to create, is more fulfilling than talking about the past for heaven's sake.

When the time comes to ask someone, "how have you been?" Instead, I prefer to say, "tell me your dreams!" It inspires a more unique conversation I'd say and helps BOTH of us have a much brighter day.

You see, everything happens because of how we are feeling. You know that positive emotions all inspire healing. Let the next words you speak be of happiness and hope, and not about how you're worried you won't cope.

There's one important piece of advice I'd like to impart … to let the power of the universe be called through your heart. Whatever you are wanting, relax your mind and allow, yourself to feel it as if you have it right now.

No longer speak of the bad stuff ... but let the good memories remain. When you live like this, things will never be the same. Our future hopes and dreams still keep calling us home, for the very best part of life, is yet to come.

CONFESSION #301 ...

I CAN IMAGINE THAT!

No matter what is happening outside, I can imagine something wonderful is behind it. I can think something incredible is really on its way to me, I can talk about all the miracles that have happened before, I can believe incredible things are about to come even more and I can know it has happened even before it walks joyfully through my door.

CONFESSION #302 ...

WHEN I NEED HELP

I stop for a moment, to take a deep breath, to feel the love in my own heart ... where help is always waiting, where peace can be sought, where stillness is found ... in any moment, through any crisis, despite any fear and in ALL ways.

CONFESSION #303 ...

I ENJOY A VARIETY OF RELATIONSHIPS

... but instead of regularly changing partners, I regularly change my behaviour, my clothing, my attitude, my outlook, my location, my personality, my habits, my needs, my mood, my desires and my proximity to my mate.

Variety is the spice of life.

Change stimulates the blossoming of growth.

Love is more delicious when I give it unconditionally.

Passion is stirred when I break the rules.

CONFESSION #304 ...

I TURN MY MAN ON BY TEASING HIM GENTLY

... with flirtatious messages, creative role playing, pretty clothing, being soft and vulnerable, being wild and free, sharing intimate fantasies, sensual photographs and the occasional cyber-sex ;-) ... but most of all I turn him on by just being me.

MY MAN TURNS ME ON WITH ROMANCE

... by taking me to different restaurants, planning trips, bringing home surprises, dedicating love songs, sending spontaneous messages, giving special gifts and daily telling me what he adores about me :-) ... but most of all he turns me on by being true to himself.

But even if he didn't do those things, I still would. I don't wait for anyone to change before I share myself in a way that makes me feel whole, loving and 100% me!

CONFESSION #305 ...

DON'T EXPECT ME TO BE YOUR FRIEND

I am NOT a friend who will follow you into the darkness to console you, to agree with your plight and keep you stuck there. But, I am someone who will shine the light for you to see, to show you a more liberating road, and to celebrate loudly as you turn the corner and drive boldly towards what you really want for your life.

CONFESSION #306 ...

THERE ARE TWO WAYS TO END A RELATIONSHIP

... by focusing on the negatives, disconnecting from my mate and from my soul (only to have the same sort of issues resurface in the next relationship).

... by focusing on the positives, staying connected to my mate and my soul (and transforming the issues for all of us).

(This confession might also be useful as a reference ... CONFESSION #272 ... WHEN A RELATIONSHIP IS MAKING ME FEEL UNCOMFORTABLE ...)

CONFESSION #307 ...

I'D LIKE TO THANK ALL THE PEOPLE WHO'VE CAUSED TROUBLE IN MY LIFE

... because you are the ones who made me expand the most, into the incredible person I am today.

CONFESSION #308 …

MY LOVE IS A GIFT

… and I expect nothing in return. What you do with that gift is entirely up to you. No matter what happens, I take each opportunity to decide who I am in spite of you, rather than finding out who I am in "response" to you … I prefer to grow in love rather than shrink in reaction!

CONFESSION #309 ...

MY PRAYERS ARE ALWAYS ANSWERED

... but instead of asking for what I don't have (giving my attention to what's missing), I say prayers of appreciation for the many ways I've already been blessed, for the incredible person I've turned out to be and for what I'm about the receive in the future, giving my undivided attention to the perfection of this precious moment.

CONFESSION #310 ...

WHEN I WANT SOMETHING WITH ALL MY HEART, ANYTHING IS POSSIBLE

I WANT TO FEEL SO GOOD ON THE INSIDE ... that no matter what other people think, I know I am amazing.

I WANT TO LOOK SO FABULOUS ON THE OUTSIDE ... that no matter what other people say, I've already decided I'm really beautiful.

I WANT TO HAVE SO MUCH EXTRA CASH ... that no matter what someone else wants, I can give it to them and know that there's plenty more where that came from.

I WANT TO SMELL SO DELICIOUS ... that the flowers turn to look at what just passed by ;-)

I WANT TO BE SO CERTAIN OF MY PERFECT HEALTH ... that no matter what the reports say, I can feel it in every cell of my body.

I WANT TO FEEL SO FREE ... that I can choose to move on, and never need to look back at where I've been.

I WANT TO SPEAK WITH SO MUCH CLARITY ... that no more words are ever necessary.

I WANT TO BE SO DETERMINED TO LIVE IN THE WAY THAT'S RIGHT FOR ME ... that I am completely unstoppable.

I WANT TO WRITE WITH SUCH CLEAR PURPOSE ... that it touches others from the inside out.

I WANT TO BE SO SURE OF WHO I AM … that what other people believe, becomes totally and utterly irrelevant.

CONFESSION #311 ...

THE ONLY TIME I RESENT SOMEONE ELSE HAVING POWER

... is when I forget that God's on my side too.

CONFESSION #312 ...

I RELEASED MY RESISTANCE TO RECEIVING

… when I realised that we are ALL worthy to have whatever we've asked for, no matter how terrible I think someone else might have been. When I stopped condemning small minded acts, I started receiving enormous rewards.

CONFESSION #313 ...

HOW OTHERS CHOOSE TO LIVE IS NONE OF MY BUSINESS

... and the less I notice what they're doing wrong, the more attention I have to give to living in the way that is right for me ... in unwavering alignment with my own integrity.

CONFESSION #314 ...

WHAT YOU THINK ABOUT ME IS NONE OF MY BUSINESS

... but what I think about you is vital.

Whenever I focus on the negative in you, I'm only noticing things I don't like ... and you usually lower yourself to prove to me that I'm right. Whenever I focus on the very best in you, I acknowledge the essence of who you really are inside ... and we both raise to meet the vibration of our combined magnificence.

CONFESSION #315 ...

WHAT MY KIDS ARE DOING IS NONE OF MY BUSINESS

I can warn them of the dangers of life, cause them to be afraid of strangers and caution them about the evils of sexual urges OR I can entrust them with the joy of life, make them aware of their own inner guidance and remind them their natural instincts define clearly when something seems right or not. One is born out of a sense of duty, the other I choose out of the depths of wisdom.

"When you give your children knowledge, you are telling them what to think. When you give your children wisdom, you do not tell them what to know, or what is true, but, rather, how to get to their own truth." - Neale Donald Walsch

CONFESSION #316 …

WHAT SOMEONE ELSE THINKS ABOUT ME IS IRRELEVANT

… what I think about MYSELF means everything.

When I'm feeling really good and someone drops out of my life it doesn't mean I've done something wrong … quite the contrary, it can mean I've just expanded so much they've forgotten who they are. I'll keep the door of my mind open in case there's something I can change, I'll keep the door of my heart open and let them find their way back, or allow someone more aligned to enter instead.

CONFESSION #317 ...

I DON'T PRACTICE BEING COMPASSIONATE ... Instead I practice "being an inspiration"

I don't join others in their dilemma. I keep my spirits raised, maintain my loving state and CALL them gently towards who I know they really want to be ... then my thoughts are naturally uplifting, my words are inspired and my actions are guided by a force far greater than you or I can fathom.

Anyone can do it ... but only when they realise that feeling bad is not the way to help anyone and that demonstration is by far the best way to teach anything.

CONFESSION #318 ...

THE CLEARER I GET ABOUT WHO I AM

… the clearer I get that there's no one right way to be.

No one life is perfect, no one moment is the ultimate, no one expression is the best, no one way of living is the right way for all ... there's just my way, and what's right for me, allowing you the space to discover your way and what's right for you!

CONFESSION #319 ...

I DECIDE WHAT I WANT FOR MY LIFE AND LIVE IT

I no longer look at other people and say "you need to change so that I can be happy".
I look at them and say, "I am so in tune with who I am, that in my eyes you are perfect!"

CONFESSION #320 ...

I LOVE TO REMEMBER LOVE

... to remember when love was blind to the faults and only had eyes for the wonder, the joy, the beauty and the passion. It doesn't only have to happen in the early part of a relationship ... it can happen for a lifetime ... when we just remember what it was really like, when our love was blind to the faults and only had eyes for the wonder, the joy, the beauty and the passion.

CONFESSION #321 ...

I DON'T CREATE THE MONEY, THE RELATIONSHIP, THE NEXT JOB OR THE NEW HOUSE

I am the creator of ME who imagines the freedom and joy that profound wealth brings, who feels the ecstasy and bliss that an intimate relationship nurtures, who attracts the most appreciative, happy and generous clients and who lives in one of the most magnificent places on the entire planet.

CONFESSION #322 …

I'M NOT IN BUSINESS TO MAKE MONEY

I do it for fun, to broaden my skills, to expand my horizons, to express my creativity, to grow my mind … and the money flows abundantly as a result.

CONFESSION #323 ...

I'M NOT ON FACEBOOK TO GET MORE FANS

I just use it for pleasure, to practise my writing, to gain enormous inspiration, to read peoples questions, to provide insight, to share what I know ... and more people and more money flow abundantly as a result.

CONFESSION #324 ...

I'M NOT IN A RELATIONSHIP SO I CAN BE LOVED

I'm in it to "flow" love on a daily basis, to give without expecting anything in return, to open my mind and heart even wider, to practise creating the relationship of my dreams and to express more deeply the love inside I know is who I am ... and as a result I feel more loved, by more people, more than words can describe.

CONFESSION #325 ...

I'M NOT HERE TO CHANGE THE WORLD

I know that it's big enough to support diversity and different ways of living. That instead of trying to fix what I "assume" are problems with other people, with corporations or with governments, that it's really my task to change what I do have control over ... my thoughts, my words, my attitudes ... and to demonstrate the peace, to live my truth, to show the acceptance and to BE the love I wish to share with the world.

CONFESSION #326 ...

I'M NOT HERE TO FIX YOU

I know you are perfect just the way you are, that you are completely worthy and no longer need to prove it, that you are loved and appreciated more than you will ever know ... and when I give you space to decide what's right for you, when I trust you're receiving your own guidance too, when I accept your uniqueness is what makes life sublime, you'll find your own way too, just as I found mine.

CONFESSION #327 ...

I LOVE LOVING

… and I look for as many reasons to love, as many things to love and as many ways to be loving, before I do anything else each day.

CONFESSION #328 ...

RELATIONSHIPS HELP ME EXPAND EVEN MORE

I WAS ALREADY HAPPY ... but choosing someone to share life with helps me find joy, meaning and purpose so much quicker.

I WAS ALREADY WISE ... but being in a relationship provides greater opportunities to open my heart and mind even wider.

I WAS ALREADY LOVED ... but the simple things we do with each other expands my understanding of intimacy even more.

I WAS ALREADY SPECIAL ... but the way he treats me lets me know I'm the most precious jewel in the world to him.

I WAS ALREADY WHOLE ... but when our bodies are entwined or his hand is holding mine, it makes me feel even more complete.

I WAS ALREADY BLESSED ... but deciding to focus on only uplifting things about each other blesses both of us beyond description.

I WAS ALREADY AT PEACE ... but when we are together, it seems as if the soft essence of God is wrapping around us all and enhances my experience of life in greater degrees than I thought possible.

CONFESSION #329 ...

I DISCOVERED HOW TO UPLIFT MY MOOD EASILY

Find something to be happy about, think about it, speak about it, write about it, tell others about it and revel in it as much as I can ... absolutely anything will do!

CONFESSION #330 …

I DISCOVERED HOW TO FEEL LOVED QUICKLY

Choose someone to love, find reasons to love them, write about the love, speak about love, do things that feel loving and revel in it as much as I can … absolutely anyone will do!

CONFESSION #331 ...

I DISCOVERED HOW TO FEEL BETTER INSTANTLY

I notice how I'm already feeling, then focus on things that feel a little better, speak about things that feel better, care only about things that feel better and care nothing about what other people are doing at all. Let how I'm feeling lead me to my own truth.

If it feels bad, it's not for me. If it feels good, it's perfectly attuned to who I prefer to be.

CONFESSION #332 ...

I DISCOVERED THE BEST WAY TO HELP SOMEONE ELSE

I don't do it by bullying them to be better, I don't do it by pointing out their weaknesses, I don't do it by showing them what they did wrong, I don't do it by expecting them to discipline themselves ... I do it by doing what I do best of all ... by accepting who they are right now, by appreciating the path they've taken to get here and by loving both of us into deeper connection with who we are becoming.

CONFESSION #333 ...

I TRUST THE LAW OF ATTRACTION

... to bring me a perfect match to what I'm REALLY thinking about, every time. Whether I've manifested illness or wellness, poverty or abundance, a loser or a lover, a rough patch or a smooth ride, it lets me know what I've been ignoring, what I've been oblivious to, what to change, what to focus upon and what to do. I appreciate this guidance more than anything.

CONFESSION #334 …

I'VE BEEN CHOSEN … to live in whatever way feels right for me … and so have YOU!

No one else can determine what's best; not my parents, not my culture, not my teachers, not my mate, not even my religion. My inner guidance holds to key to ALL the goodness that life has to offer. No matter what I've done in the past, no decision was ever wrong … some decisions are just more aligned with "who I really am" and where I intend to take my life.

CONFESSION #335 ...

OH WOW, I'VE WON THE LOTTERY

I'm so excited about what I've already been given, the life I've lived, the places I've been, the things I've done, the friends I've met and the opportunities I've taken, that it feels as if I've won the greatest prize ... the prize of deep emotional fulfilment, positive mental upliftment and expansive heartfelt joy ... and I'm eager to experience even more of what the universe has in store for me.

CONFESSION #336 …

LIFE IS EASY FOR ME

… especially when I use my mind to focus on where I want to go, when I use my heart to show me the way, when I use my feelings to know if I'm on track and when I use the powers of the universe to bring me everything my mind decides, my feelings define and my heart desires.

I always get what I want … in the very moment I release the resistance to receiving it!

CONFESSION #337 ...

I DON'T ALWAYS BELIEVE YOU

... I only choose to believe things that uplift, enhance, expand and liberate both of us.

CONFESSION #338 ...

I DECIDE WHAT LIFE MEANS TO ME

I love getting bills ... because it means I have the money to pay them.
I love having issues ... because it means I have the ability to overcome them.
I love hearing a different opinion ... because it means I have an opportunity to change my mind.
I love disagreements ... because it means I have the chance to better focus my thoughts.
I love being confronted ... because it means I can make a choice to be happy or be right.
I love getting sick ... because it means I have a bigger reason to concentrate on things that make me feel better.
I love the occasional heart ache ... because it means I have the capacity to expand into unconditional love and feel even more empowered than I did before.

The key to a happy life isn't to manipulate the conditions around me so I can feel better, the key is to change the "meaning" I give it and feel happy no matter what happens.

CONFESSION #339 ...

I LOOKED FOR LOVE IN ALL THE WRONG PLACES

... I thought my mate should change so I could love him more. I expected my kids to behave so they were worthy of my praise. I though YOU should believe the same things I do so I could shower you with blessings ... but I was wrong. That's not real love – that's conditional love.

I DECIDED TO LOVE ANYWAY!

... to accept others just the way they are no matter what they were thinking, to praise the essence of each person I meet no matter what they were doing, to bless you no matter what you believe ... not because you deserve it, not because it's the right thing to do, not because I'll go to heaven when I die, but because it's the best way I know to BE THE LOVE THAT IS ME.

CONFESSION #340 ...

I LIKE IT THAT YOU LOVE ME

… but most of all, I love it when YOU LOVE YOU.

CONFESSION #341 ...

ONE DAY I JUST STOPPED CARING

... about what other people might think about who I am, what I'm doing and where I'm at ... and then fell completely, totally and utterly in love with the person I know inside is really me.

CONFESSION #342 ...

THE PERFECT MATE

... is the one I'm with, the one who waits for me, the one who's the most obvious, because Law Of Attraction always brings me whatever is in harmony with my dominant thoughts, beliefs, conversations and attitudes ... and when those things change, my mate will either transform in front of my eyes or will gently drift away allowing another to perfectly fill the space.

CONFESSION #343 ...

I'M A PLAYER

Life is meant to be fun, to be heart warming, to be enjoyed, to be lived to the fullest.

I regularly get involved in games like "Find the positive aspects of this person", "How many genuine compliments can I pay", "What's the most uplifting thing I can say", "Seek the blessing in this situation", but one of my favourite games of all is "Appreciating everything I've already been given!"

CONFESSION #344 ...

YOU CAN'T STOP ME

… from loving the essence of who you really are …. but there are things that you can think, say and do that resist or enhance the natural energy flow between us, that either push us further apart or bring us closer together.

CONFESSION #345 ...

I LOVE FEELING MY EMOTIONS

Everything I do is designed to make me feel something ...

... playing sport, having kids, getting into a relationship, going to the movies, becoming involved in someone else's drama, creating my own, going somewhere different, going somewhere familiar, picking a fight, starting a business, buying a new house, watching TV, meditating etc.

When I am feeling ANYTHING, I know I'm truly alive!

CONFESSION #346 ...

MY CONFESSIONS HELP ME GET TO KNOW MYSELF BETTER

They are notes to myself, not to God, not to a lawyer, not to a court and are not intended to impact anyone else, yet when I'm expanding my heart, when I'm opening my mind, when I'm growing in spirit, the people around me seem to expand, open, grow and benefit enormously as well.

CONFESSION #347 ...

I DIDN'T GET INTO A GREAT RELATIONSHIP BY WAITING FOR THE RIGHT PERSON TO SHOW UP

… I got into a great relationship by experiencing and practicing my way there and by becoming the sort of person who appreciates the growth and expansion that ALL relationships offer.

CONFESSION #348 ...

I DIDN'T GET BETTER HEALTH BY WAITING FOR THE RIGHT MIRACLE CURE

… I got better healthy by relaxing my way there, and by becoming someone who chooses to remember my spiritual wellbeing, notices my emotional state and tends lovingly to my mental focus, no matter what might have manifested physically.

CONFESSION #349 ...

I DIDN'T GET INCREASED WEALTH BY WAITING FOR THE RIGHT LOTTERY NUMBERS TO BE DRAWN

… I got increased wealth by playing and enjoying my way there, and by becoming someone who appreciates ALL that I have in my life right now and excitedly anticipates even more in the future.

CONFESSION #350 ...

I DIDN'T FIND SUCCESS BY LOOKING FOR IT

... I became successful by being true to my own desires and letting the good things in life find me.

CONFESSION #351 ...

I DON'T GET WHAT I WANT BY FIGHTING FOR IT

... I stay silent, stay positive, stay aligned and allow it to manifest in its own way, in its own time and with results that amaze even me. Fighting is fraught with resistance. Allowing, trusting and believing is an indication I am in pure alignment with everything I've ever wished for.

CONFESSION #352 …

I DON'T HAVE A GREAT LIFE BECAUSE EVERYTHING GOES WELL

… I just accept that life has its ups and downs and choose to find creative ways to turn the 'shit' into valuable fertiliser anyway.

CONFESSION #353 ...

I DIDN'T FIND MY PLACE IN THE WORLD BY TAKING THE ADVICE OF OTHERS

... I let the right way unfold naturally by noticing what brings me relief, what feels so much better, what makes me really happy, what fills me with passion, what energises me to action, what leads me to joy, what lights up my life and then by moving with gentle persistence towards even more of it.

CONFESSION #354 ...

I DON'T GET THROUGH MY PROBLEMS BY WORKING ON THEM

... I spend time appreciating what's already going well in my life and allow what isn't, to transform gently into solutions.

CONFESSION #355 ...

I DIDN'T GAIN RESPECT BY COMMANDING IT

… respect came naturally when instead of speaking my mind, I speak from the heart!

CONFESSION #356 ...

I DON'T GET WHAT I WANT BY IMPLEMENTING AN ACTION PLAN

… I take time to attune my thoughts, my attitudes, my words and my vibration, into believing it's already done, and when I feel good about that, the right action is divinely inspired with no agenda in mind.

The universe always gives me what I ask for, but it doesn't just hear my words, think my thoughts or know my action … it feels my emotional vibration and gives me exactly what I'm putting out.

I TAKE ACTION

… but only when it feels right, when it's inspired and when the energy is impossible to contain. That's when I get the most amazing results, without forcing, without trying to manipulate anyone else or the laws of the universe AND without any extra effort at all. Life was meant to be easy.

CONFESSION #357 ...

I DIDN'T GET HAPPY BY EXPECTING OTHER PEOPLE TO CHANGE

… I got happy by changing my own thoughts, words and actions and by bringing them into harmony with who I know inside we all really are … magnificent souls all doing the very best we can in each blessed moment.

CONFESSION #358 …

I DON'T HAVE A GREAT NIGHT OUT BECAUSE I'VE CHOSEN THE RIGHT ENVIRONMENT, THE RIGHT FRIENDS AND THE RIGHT CLOTHES

… I enjoy myself immensely just by focusing on the best parts of life, no matter where I am, who I'm with and how I look.

CONFESSION #359 ...

I DON'T NEED TO MAKE THINGS HAPPEN

… Life gets easier every time I STOP trying to "make" things happen and start focusing on what I WANT to experience and why I want to experience it. There's often a better road that takes me towards my desires and when I trust it will be shown to me, the way is always paved immaculately before me.

CONFESSION #360 …

I CAN'T ARGUE WITH SOMEONE AND BRING US CLOSER

I can only find harmony with my thoughts, remember the good things about our relationship, focus on the aspects that I love the most, connect closer to my own soul and keep open the flow of loving energy that brought us together in the first place. In this way I keep my vibration pure and allow my heart to call forward even better things in the future.

CONFESSION #361 ...

I HAVE THE BEST GUY IN THE WORLD

His support is life-giving, his love is so generously shared, his willingness to grow with me is amazing, his desire for us to be together strengthens me, his body entwined with mine feels completely divine ... and if he wasn't already these things and more, my genuine acknowledgement of them would magnetize the best parts towards me anyway.

CONFESSION #362 …

I KNOW MY OWN POWER

… it's the ability I have inside me to notice the best, to openly acknowledge the best and to manifest the best in others … and in myself. As much as the world wants to believe success is about finding the best job, the best mentor, the best home, the best friends, the best mate, it has everything to do with me believing that I AM the best person first and foremost.

CONFESSION #363 ...

I CARE ABOUT ME FIRST

No one ever questions whether my actions are genuine; no one ever wonders if I mean what I say. There's no agenda, no trying to achieve a particular result, no wanting to manipulate an outcome ... whatever I do comes from my heart, whatever I give is given with love and whatever I say is said with truth.

CONFESSION #364 ...

I NO LONGER CARE ABOUT WHAT I'M GETTING

… I only focus on what I'm giving, how I'm doing and who I'm being. What I'm getting is simply an indication of what I've been expecting. What I'm giving is an indication of how good I'm feeling about myself … and I feel fabulous!

CONFESSION #365 ...

THE BEST SOLUTIONS COME WHEN I RELAX

When I get frustrated with my problems, I often take action that's ineffective just to relieve the pain. But when I relax and trust my higher guidance will deliver the answer, more positive thoughts are drawn, the right words are spoken, the best actions are inspired and the clearest truth is discovered.

CONFESSION #366 ...

MY PLAN FOR SUCCESS

GET RELIEF from whatever is bothering me, in whatever way I can (without judgment).

EXPRESS HOW I'M REALLY FEELING and then spend endless time doing whatever it takes to feel a little better, moment by moment.

LOOK FOR THE BLESSING IN EACH SITUATION

FIND SOMETHING TO APPRECIATE (anything at all will do).

CHOOSE SOMEONE TO LOVE and then flow as much love as possible towards that person, (not because I want something in return, but because it feels REALLY GOOD to love, from the inside out).

LOVE MYSELF MORE TOO. When I love me, I have so much more to give others.

GIVE MYSELF A BREAK

GIVE EVERYONE ELSE A BREAK. Stop expecting them to meet my needs and meet my own instead.

THINK ABOUT, TALK ABOUT AND DO THINGS THAT FEEL GOOD, and gently let go of the things that don't.

BE AUTHENTIC. Follow my bliss. Live the life that's right for me, in tune with my own integrity.

CONFESSION #367 ...

I KNOW HOW WE FALL IN AND OUT OF LOVE ...

"Falling in love" is the sensation we feel when we surrender to fully opening our hearts and minds, choose to love unconditionally and re-connect to our own soul. We often "attach" this FEELING to the other person, experience or object that stimulated it ... but they are simply the catalyst ... We were all born to love and when we choose to do so without expecting anything in return, we remember who we really are at the core of our being.

We "fall out of love" by doing a similar thing in reverse ... and often mistakenly attach to our mate, the unpleasant sensation we feel when we've closed our hearts and minds and placed conditions on our love ... but the other person is simply the catalyst ... and we are using them as our excuse for not feeling the connection to our soul and being the incredibly loving person we know in our hearts is who we were always meant to be.

CONFESSION #368 ...

I AM FREE

… and you are free to be whoever we choose to be.

CONFESSION #369 ...

I AM SO DETERMINED

When I get determined about something, rather than deciding what I want to do or have, I decide WHO I intend to be.

I am determined to BE someone who finds the blessing no matter what might be happening, someone who loves no matter what other people are doing, someone who believes in myself no matter what other people are saying and someone whose connection to their own inner knowing is greater than ANY problem!

CONFESSION #370 …

I KNOW WHERE I'M GOING

… but I rarely decide exactly how I'll get there.

"My Creator" is forever calling me towards the places I've already wished to go. I just listen to my heart, use my mind to stay positively focused and allow my emotions to tell me if I'm getting closer to or further from what is already waiting for me to graciously accept it as mine.

CONFESSION #371 ...

I ONCE CLAIMED I WANTED WORLD PEACE

... but when I really thought about it, I would have been condemning someone else's choices in order to get it.

That's not real peace, that's conditional righteousness. Now I prefer to claim the "peace in my heart" which starts as an inner journey which I choose to take quietly, as often as I can, knowing that the ripple effect will gently impact others.

CONFESSION #372 ...

I TRUST MY FEELINGS

They tell me immediately if something feels off or if it feels pleasant. When I don't value my own feelings and opt to take someone else's advice instead, I move away from my natural nature, ignore my gut instincts and lose a sense of "who I really am". Most people end up searching the rest of their lives trying to find themselves again. If it feels good, if it feels right, if it makes my heart sing ... it's right for ME!

CONFESSION #373 ...

I TREAT LIFE AS A GREAT ADVENTURE

... so that when I run out of fuel on a country road in the middle of a cool winters night, I imagine it as being great entertainment while I wait for someone to rescue me in the morning. I've found that humour has much greater power to solve problems than trying to think my way out will ever do.

CONFESSION #374 ...

I KNOW HOW TO GET THE LOVE OF MY LIFE TO COME BACK

I can get him back in an instant by IMAGINING being with him right now, by thinking about the happy times we shared, by remembering the wonderful things we enjoyed, by feeling the love I have in this moment, by planning to be with him into the future .... and to also allow the space for someone who will always be there for me, to come along instead.

But MOST IMPORTANTLY, I can find that blissful connection I have to my own sense of self and bring it to the forefront so strongly, that I become "the love of my own life".

From there, magic happens.

CONFESSION #375 ...

I'M REALLY POWERFUL

While most people think that power is the ability to influence or control others ... to me, real power is when I recognize instinctively that no situation is bad enough, no government is strong enough and no other person is manipulative enough to take away, change or misrepresent who I really am inside.

CONFESSION #376 ...

LIFE IS FOR MY PLEASURE ... so I please myself first!

... not my mate, not my family, not my parents, not my peers.

The more I try to do things for others instead of doing them for me, the more out of alignment I become and the more dependent on me they become. It doesn't seem to matter what I do, some people just refuse to be happy. Today I ask myself "how do I really want to please myself most of all?"

CONFESSION #377 ...

I CHANGED MY LIFE ... BY CHANGING MY FOCUS

All my problems are just an indication of my past thoughts, beliefs, complaints, attitudes and expectations, which means I can change what's happening almost instantly by focusing whole-heartedly on what I really want to experience instead. Hallelujah!

CONFESSION #378 ...

I BELIEVE IN YOU

The poor don't want to be treated like paupers, the sick don't want to be treated like invalids, the weak don't want to be treated like weaklings ... we all respond so much better when someone believes in our capabilities, has faith that we can solve our own problems and reminds us of the innate strength, love and fortitude contained in our own spirit.

CONFESSION #379 ...

WHEN I WANT BETTER RESULTS

I make peace with where I am before I make a new decision.

I think positive thoughts before I act,

I feel centered before I start the next conversation,

I find contentment before I reach for some comfort food,

I acknowledge my freedom before I make another commitment,

I get "in my happy place" first and then do that exercise, feel loving and make love!

CONFESSION #380 ...

I DON'T WORRY

Worrying is just like begging to experience more of the things I don't want.

BUT I DO HAVE FAITH THAT GOOD THINGS ARE ON THEIR WAY TO ME

I keep on appreciating the things I consciously choose to believe are already mine until I know them so well, they simply become real.

CONFESSION #381 ...

I'M NOT RESPONSIBLE FOR THE WAY YOU FEEL

… that's your job! And you're not responsible for the way I feel either … It's up to me to focus my thoughts, to give my attention and uplift my spirits in ways that feel good. I can be dependent on you to make me happy or I can set us free to give unconditionally, when it just feels right for you and for me.

CONFESSION #382 …

NOTHING YOU DO CAN AFFECT ME NEGATIVELY FOR VERY LONG

… unless I keep on giving it my attention, keep complaining about it, keep on making you "wrong" for doing it AND foolishly forget that I have my own life to live ;-)

CONFESSION #383 ...

I'M A BELIEVER

… I don't doubt that the power of this awesome universe can make "anything" possible.

CONFESSION #384 ...

IT'S EASY TO LOVE PEOPLE WHO AGREE WITH ME

… but it enhances my experience of life so much more when I also choose to accept, value, respect and appreciate those who don't.

CONFESSION #385 ...

WHEN I FELL IN LOVE

... it was never really about the other person. They just stimulated me to open my heart, to flourish, to thrive and to amplify who I already know myself to be.

WHEN I FELL "OUT OF LOVE"

... it was never really about the other person either. But instead of using them as an excuse to close my heart, to shrink in reaction, to die inside, I've decided to use them as a reason to grow into a more enhanced version of who I really am: a natural born lover, a giver, an uplifter and a vibrant liver of life.

CONFESSION #386 …

I DON'T NEED TO CHOOSE THE QUALITIES I WANT IN A MATE

… I just decide what qualities I intend to develop in myself and let the law of attraction take care of the rest. Yeeeeeeeeeees!

CONFESSION #387 ...

THE HARDEST THINGS CAN BE THE MOST REWARDING

TO ACCEPT ... even when I felt like condemning.

TO LOVE ... even when my heart was hurting.

TO BELIEVE IN MYSELF ... even when others doubted my abilities.

TO FIND STRENGTH ... even when all hope was lost.

TO EXPRESS MY FEELINGS ... even when I was afraid of the result.

TO TRUST MY INNER GUIDANCE ... even though I was feeling stuck.

TO GO FOR WHAT I REALLY WANTED ... even though it seemed unreasonable.

TO ALLOW MYSELF TO BE VULNERABLE ... even when I was crying out for certainty.

TO HAVE FAITH THAT EVERYTHING IS WORKING OUT PERFECTLY ... even if it seemed far from the truth.

TO KNOW IT'S OK TO BE WHERE I'M AT ... because this too will change, even if I don't know the answer, even if I haven't found clarity, even if I'm not yet aware of the solution and even if I do nothing at all.

CONFESSION #388 ...

I'M NOT BEING TESTED

I'm being shown, where my attitude was misaligned so that I can choose the attitude I want instead.

CONFESSION #389 ...

I DON'T NEED TO BE PROTECTED

The more I protect myself from experiencing pain, the less opportunity I get to focus my mind, to decide what I want instead, to set my intention, to direct my life in more powerful ways. Moving through problems creates the greatest opportunity to grow my spirit, to expand my mind and live more fully than I've ever done before.

CONFESSION #390 …

SOMETIMES I NEED TO DISTRACT MYSELF

… from thinking about what's happening, from concentrating on the past, from focusing on what's wrong, from conversations that bring me down … and move towards what feels better, to the things that uplift my spirits, to the light of love that always calls me to open my heart and be the inspiring leader I was born to be.

CONFESSION #391 ...

I HAVE A NEW DREAM

… and I just keep on dreaming new dreams, not because I'm avoiding reality, not because I hope they'll come true, not because of the results I might get in the end, but because it feels SO VERY GOOD to dream. Do you remember how good it feels too?

CONFESSION #392 ...

I DON'T MAKE MY DREAMS COME TRUE

I just don't contradict them with doubt or by sharing them with people who don't understand the process. Instead, I allow them to create a life of their own and just move with curiosity, eagerness, interest and gentle persistence towards them.

CONFESSION #393 ...

YOU CAN'T HARASS ME INTO BEING A BETTER PERSON

You can't discipline me into doing what's right.

You can't make rules that place me on a safer path.

You can't point out my weakness and bring out my strengths.

You can't demand that I change and have it be a lasting one ...

... so I'm going to stop doing it to others!

CONFESSION #394 ...

I HAVE LEARNED ... that it's best to open my heart before I open my mouth.

What comes out is more likely to light up someones life rather than add fuel to the fire!

CONFESSION #395 ...

I CHANGED MY ATTITUDE AND CHANGED MY LIFE

I used to say that life was a struggle, then I realized that this attitude made it seem even harder. Now I imagine that life is fantastic and notice how this attitude lightens my mood, attracts more great stuff and inspires others to feel better as well.

CONFESSION #396 ...

THERE REALLY ARE NO LIES

... just what each person thinks, believes, repeats, speaks about, affirms, expects, declares, acknowledges, loves or appreciates into existence.

CONFESSION #397...

I'LL GET WHAT I WANT IN THE END

… whether I have to die to get to heaven or live like it exists here on earth.

CONFESSION #398...

I APPRECIATE WHERE I AM, WHAT I AM AND WHO I AM

... Right here! Right now!

CONFESSION #399...

THERE ARE THREE WAYS TO LIVE MY LIFE

1. HOPE that if I'm careful enough, nothing bad will happen.

2. BELIEVE that if I'm good enough, God will take care of me.

3. KNOW that all the resources of the universe are on my side and I'll find a way, no matter what happens.

CONFESSION #400 ...

THINGS KEEP GETTING BETTER ...

Whenever I stay silent instead of complain, as I release the bad but let the good memories remain.
Every time I overlook an issue to see the deeper intent, when I take a moment to understand what they really meant.
Things keep getting better as I learn to trust, that there's nothing I need do even when I assume that I must.
It happens naturally with each thought I improve, with each wrong that I right, when I look towards peace instead of turning to fight, and as I move through the darkness and shine my light bright.

CONFESSION #401 ...

SOMETIMES I ENJOY FEELING SAD

... so I can make myself feel better again.

CONFESSION #402 ...

BEING LOVING AND CONTENTED GETS BORING AFTER A WHILE

… and I enjoy getting hooked into some drama so I can feel my emotions more fully, and then choose again those which I intend to experience the most.

CONFESSION #403 ...

I HAVE THE POWER TO INFLUENCE OTHERS

… but I don't do it with negative feedback, instead I use positive reinforcement.

I know so surely that you are an amazing being, that as time goes by you'll come to know it too!

I feel so good about who we both are, that within a short space of time, you'll be feeling good too.

I see so clearly that we are ALL beautiful souls, that pretty soon you'll ALL be able to see it too.

CONFESSION #404...

LIFE GIVES ME ENDLESS CHANCES

… to recreate who I once was, to try something new, to make a different choice.

It matters not what I've done, how much struggle I've faced or how many mistakes I've made … there's always another opportunity to start again and experience even greater delights than ever before.

Death provides me with the same opportunity too.

CONFESSION #405 ...

I KNOW THAT I LIVE FOREVER

... and that there's more to life and death than meets the eye.

CONFESSION #406 ...

I CAN'T COMPLAIN ABOUT SOMETHING AND MAKE MYSELF FEEL BETTER

The best I can do is imagine the blessings that could be born from the experience and feel good about that instead.

CONFESSION #407 ...

I CAN'T DEMAND THAT OTHER PEOPLE CHANGE AND REALLY MAKE IT HAPPEN

... the best I can do is BE the change and inspire others to follow.

CONFESSION #408 ...

I AM FOREVER ASKING QUESTIONS

I have an insatiable need to know more, to expand my mind, to improve who I already am, but the question I once asked the most when times got tough, "what the hell did I do wrong this time?" has now been replaced with more empowering ones like,

What do I really want?

Why do I want it?

What will help me feel better than I do right now?

What am I happy about today?

What do I appreciate today?

What have I done well today?

Is this who I really am?

I now ask questions that draw a more inspiring response.

CONFESSION #409 ...

NOTHING FEELS BETTER THAN WHEN I LOVE

... just because I can!

CONFESSION #410 ...

I'VE GOT EVERYTHING I NEED

The answers to my questions are waiting for me to remember them. The solutions to my problems are waiting for me to "allow" them. The clarity to my confusion is waiting to be revealed to me and everything I've ever wished to receive is contained right here in the communion of my heart, mind and soul, where it's been all along.

CONFESSION #411 ...

THE ONLY FAILURE

… is when I fail to find ways to feel a little better, when I fail to focus on something that brings relief, when I fail to aim for hope in any situation, when I fail to only speak well of myself and others, when I fail to do what's right for me no matter what other people might think.

CONFESSION #412 ...

THERE ARE THREE TYPES OF ACTION I CAN TAKE:

1. PREPARE for the worst and protect myself.

2. FORCE myself to take action and hope for the best.

3. ALIGN my thoughts, words and beliefs with what I want for my life and then be inspired to action.

CONFESSION #413 ...

I THINK YOU ARE PERFECT JUST THE WAY YOU ARE

While most people expect others to behave in certain ways, I just want you to be YOU, no matter where you're at, no matter what it might look like, no matter how negative it might be ... because I KNOW you'll feel your naturally loving, kind and respectful self really soon, without me demanding that you get there right now! The more I allow you to just BE you, the more I allow me to just BE me too – authentic and real.

I JUST WANT YOU TO BE "YOU" IN YOUR AUTHENTIC AND REAL STATE

... not some contrived person like our parents, our teachers, our culture or our religion taught us to be. Just be who you really are, express where you're really at, and I know that pretty soon, you'll be feeling your magnificent self, all over again.

CONFESSION #414 ...

I ALLOW THE GOOD THINGS IN LIFE TO HAPPEN NATURALLY

I just let go the thought, avoid saying the words or stop doing the action that prevents it. I usually know what it is, because I've done it time and time again. All I need is a willingness to change an old pattern/habit that no longer supports who I am now becoming.

CONFESSION #415 ...

THE MOST REWARDING THING I'VE EVER DONE

… is when I decided to be kind to someone even though they weren't being kind to me, when I allowed someone their freedom even though they tried to take away mine, when I kept on loving even though I thought my heart was breaking, when I gave more of what I had to offer even though I'd already given enough.

In that moment I discovered "I AM ENOUGH".

CONFESSION #416 ...

I'M EASILY TURNED ON

... when I open my heart.

I'M QUICKLY TUNED IN

... when I open my mind.

I'M THOROUGHLY WIRED UP

... when I bare my soul.

CONFESSION #417 ...

I'M DELUSIONAL

I can find the good in everything - in life and in death, in elation and in depression, in peace and in terrorism, in nature and in a natural disaster ... and even in the government ;-)

CONFESSION #418 ...

SOME PEOPLE THINK I HAVE STRANGE IDEAS

I take is as a delightful compliment. They thought Christopher Columbus was strange when he was convinced he could sail off a flat world. There are major changes taking place on this planet right now, and amongst it all, there is nothing more moving than an idea "whose time has come!"

CONFESSION #419 ...

I WONDER?

Will these words hurt you or enlighten,
Give you comfort or be confronting?
Will they CAUSE you to react or stimulate deep thinking?
Will you decide they are 'abusive' or see the real intent
or
Perhaps they'll mean nothing and you'll let them pass by instead.
When we rise above reactions we see loves' deeper glow,
For without someone to push us there'd be no opportunity to grow.

CONFESSION #420 ...

I NEVER GAVE UP

When I felt like giving up – I gave more.
When I felt like closing down – I opened up.
When I felt like letting go – I held on.
When I felt like running away – I committed again.
When I felt like I wanted to die – I learned how to live again and the rewards were phenomenal!

CONFESSION #421 ...

THERE ARE THINGS I JUST WON'T DO

If a thought doesn't feel good ... then I won't think it!

If a conversation doesn't sound uplifting ... then I won't get involved in it!

If a news story doesn't make me happy ... then I won't watch it!

If a belief limits my potential ... then I stop repeating it!

What I focus on gets bigger, so I choose to focus on how I want my life to be instead.

CONFESSION #422 ...

THERE'S ONLY ONE WAY TO MAKE SOMETHING, GO AWAY

Most of us were brought up to believe that if we disapproved of something, fought against something or kept saying "NO" to something, we'd make it go away. But the only way to really make something we don't like "go away" is to take our attention AWAY from it.

OUT OF SIGHT, OUT OF MIND, OUT OF EXPERIENCE

Instead, I focus on my passions, focus on feeling good, focus on uplifting others, focus on finding hope, focus on having great sex, focus on sharing love, focus on cooking a delicious meal, focus on making peace with my neighbour, focus on smiling at the next person I meet ... they are the things that make a REAL difference in this world!

CONFESSION #423 ...

BRING IT ON! ... I can handle anything!

Something that happens might throw me off track for a while, but as I keep training my focus towards a solution instead of complaining about the problem, the law of attraction awards me with an even greater prize ... inner peace AND outer manifestations ... thank you.

CONFESSION #424 ...

MY JOB DESCRIPTION

My job is to uplift others, not to point out their weaknesses.

My job is to turn negative perceptions into life giving ones.

My job is to give hope where hope has been lost.

My job is to talk about what's possible, not to agree about what others think is impossible.

My job is to spread good news, not to regurgitate the bad.

My job is to encourage each persons uniqueness, not to resolve differences.

My job is to celebrate individuality, not to promote sameness.

My job is to soothe you into loving yourself more, to inspire you to remember the precious connection to your higher self, to see your incredible magnificence reflected in the eyes of everyone else and assist you to align with your own soul.

CONFESSION #425 ...

I WON'T CHANGE JUST TO PLEASE YOU

Whenever I change who I am so someone else can feel better, I stop giving them a reason to grow and weaken my own spirit.

Whenever I stay true to myself despite how someone else is reacting, I grant them an opportunity to grow and strengthen our combined souls.

CONFESSION #426 ...

WHEN MY RELATIONSHIP IS FALLING APART

… it isn't my mate who needs to change, it isn't me that needs to be fixed, it's the relationship I have with myself that needs some adjustment. As I spend more time in my happy and contented place, my mate will either realign and join me, OR someone more compatible will feel compelled to enter. Whatever happens, we all win.

CONFESSION #427 …

RELATIONSHIPS GIVE ME MORE OPPORTUNITY FOR SPIRITUAL GROWTH

I don't expect longevity, I don't expect my mate to make me happy, I don't expect myself to behave impeccably, I don't expect things to always go perfectly … what I do expect is that I will keep my relationship with myself as aligned and authentic as possible. I am a lover and uplifter, who chooses to live mostly in joy and with eagerness to experience more of life and love from all perspectives.

CONFESSION #428 ...

THINGS ARE GETTING BETTER ALL THE TIME

Each day as I overcome another obstacle, uncover another blessing, discover something new, experience something different, open my mind, grow my heart, try again, ... I become MORE of who I already am ... Life can't shrink me, it can only expand my potential.

CONFESSION #429 ...

I DON'T LET ANYONE BECOME DEPENDENT ON ME

... for their answers, for their finances, for love or for their alignment. YOU have your own answers, your own guidance, your own creativity, your own intuition, your own good ideas and your own loving essence inside of you. Dependency contracts our experience of life, love sets others free to experience life for themselves, and grow into the magnificent beings they were born to be.

CONFESSION #430 ...

I KNOW THE BENEFIT OF CONTRAST

Out of discomfort, a way to be more comfortable is conceived.

Out of rejection, a way to accept our own uniqueness is attained.

Out of hurt, a way to feel soothed is found.

Out of want, a way to achieve our hearts desire is defined.

Out of pain, a way to get relief is sought.

Out of death, a way to prolong quality of life is produced.

Out of disaster, a way to provide safer conditions is discovered.

Out of all contrast comes the ability to expand, to grow, to evolve and to give life its ultimate purpose ... to continue to infinity and beyond.

CONFESSION #431 ...

I CAN UNDERSTAND THE CYCLE OF LIFE

When my heart has a desire and I follow it, I feel good.

If my mind gets in the way of my desire, I feel pain.

The pain is an indication my thoughts are off track, I look for relief.

Getting relief helps me relax my old patterns of thought, so

I can change my mind and choose again.

Making a new choice gets me back on the path to following my heart.

When my heart has a new desire and I follow it, I feel good!

CONFESSION #432 ...

I CHANGE MY MIND WHENEVER I FEEL LIKE IT

… and know there is great power in lining up my energy, my thoughts, my attitude and my beliefs in to be consistent NOT with the person I was yesterday, but in alignment with the person I am intending to become tomorrow.

CONFESSION #433 ...

I CHOOSE MY OWN DESTINY

I am the decider of my fate, I am the director of my life, I am the creator of my reality.

I am the attractor of what might appear to be luck, I am valued by the divine, I am attuned to infinite intelligence and my life is solely mine.

There is nothing outside of me that can meddle with my vibration, there's just a loving energy that's been gifted to me, to thoughtfully weave into my own creation.

CONFESSION #434 ...

I LOVE GETTING PAID FOR JUST BEING ME

... for just being here, for just being alive, for just doing what I do best ... being an uplifter, living an inspired life, providing unconditional acceptance of where each person is at, consistently shining my light and flowing love through and from my eternal soul.

Authenticity is the biggest game in town.

CONFESSION #435 ...

SOMETIMES CHANGE IS UNCOMFORTABLE

My heart's a flutter, my stomach is churning,
I can feel my vibration raising and a deeper passion burning.
My emotions are here to show me, if I'm moving further or getting close,
to the strong desires I set in motion each time I'd been hurt the most.

Sometimes it feels uncomfortable, to leave the past behind,
so many people share my journey and they've all helped me define,
the things that mean so much, the things I want for me,
the things that fire my inner spark and set my spirit free.

CONFESSION #436 ...

I DID IT MY WAY ... and I wouldn't change a thing.

CONFESSION #437 ...

I USE MY IMAGINATION

I use my imagination to feel anything at will, to rock my boat, to give me a thrill.
To gently think of things that bring me more ease, to find relief, to feel at peace.
I use my imagination to raise my vibration, to generate intense pleasure, focus on loving sensations.
I use my imagination to play with prosperity, to speak well on stage, to enhance creativity,
to remind me that things can be as I want them to be, instead of just accepting mere reality.

CONFESSION #438 ...

SOMETIMES I CAN'T RESPOND WITH LOVE

… because I've moved so far away from my peaceful centre … but that's OK! I allow myself to respond in whatever way feels appropriate and then move step by step towards that peaceful centre once again.

Revenge feels better than powerlessness.
Anger feels better than depression.
Blame feels better than guilt.
Being negative feels better than being worried.
Getting laid is probably the best remedy of all … lol

… and finding something to laugh about beats everything.

CONFESSION #439 ...

I LOVE MYSELF SO MUCH

… and as I align with my higher nature, attune myself to the oneness, as I fill up with more joy, with even greater appreciation, when I focus on my most exhilarating passions and find deeper internal peace, then The Universe carves out the perfect relationships for me … and it places me on a kind path, a loving path, a liberating path and everybody benefits profoundly because of it.

CONFESSION #440 ...

SOMETIMES I NEED TO REMIND MYSELF WHO I REALLY AM ...

I am loving, I am beautiful, I am joyful, I am kind, I am expansive, I am radiant, I have peace and clarity of mind.

I am magnetic, I am creative, I am receptive, I am inspiring, I am original, I am abundant, I am graceful, I am amazing.

I am magnificent, I am protected, I am served and I'm adored, I am treasured, I am admired and I am supported even more.

I am grateful, I am magical, I am power, I am light, I am appreciative, I am valuable, I am wisdom, I have insight.

I am passion and inspiration and content I love to be, I am in the flow, I am wealthy, I am wise, I am ME!

I am present, I am fulfilled, I am perfectly complete. My emotions are empowering, from the heart I like to speak.

My body, mind and spirit are in total harmony.
I am blissful, I am ecstatic, I am healthy, I am FREE.

CONFESSION #441 ...

I HAVE A STRONG DESIRE

… and find it empowering when I hold a vision in my mind of who I know someone really is, despite the behaviour they may be currently exhibiting … and shine the light so brightly for them that they can do nothing else but see it too.

CONFESSION #442 ...

I LOVE THE ONE I'M WITH; UNTIL I ATTRACT THE ONE I LOVE

Withholding my love hurts no one but me,
because I'm not being the incredible person that I came here to be.
Staying open and being loving is the most fulfilling action,
giving all I have to give and trusting the law of attraction;
to always bring the perfect match to my vibration,
and a mate who harmonizes wholly with my emanation.

CONFESSION #443 ...

I DON'T CONTROL WHAT HAPPENS ... but I can influence it!

Even if I could control the other people and circumstances in my LIFE ... I wouldn't want to! Life would be boring and predictable. So I take care of what I can control - my responses, my thoughts, my attitude, my proximity to the problem and where I focus my attention. There's incredible power in doing that.

CONFESSION #444 …

I HAVE THE DEEPEST LOVE AND APPRECIATION

… for my higher self/GOD/universal energy, for inspiring the words, expanding the wisdom, answering profound questions, providing eternal solutions and ever so brightly guiding my path.

CONFESSION #445 ...

JUST WHEN I WAS WONDERING IF LIFE WAS GONNA GET ANY BETTER ... it did!

I found ways to open my heart in the face of rejection. I loved beyond boundaries I'd previously set. I experienced an inner power that far exceeded anything I'd felt before. Nothing in my exterior world changed ... just the gentle allowance of my souls' desire to combine in harmony with the majestic forces of the entire universe.

CONFESSION #446 …

WHEN I'M GOOD, I'M VERY, VERY GOOD

… and when I'm not, I just have an opportunity to get better.

CONFESSION #447 ...

MY PERSONAL MISSION STATEMENT

I treat every person I encounter like someone I love dearly - no exceptions.
If I wouldn't THINK something about my loved one, I won't think it about anyone else.
If I wouldn't SAY something to or about my loved one, I won't say it to or about anyone else.
If I wouldn't DO something to my loved one, I won't do it to anyone else.

CONFESSION #448 ...

I DON'T CARE WHAT'S RIGHT OR WRONG

I only care for how I feel about what I'm thinking, doing, or saying in each moment. I'm not the judge and jury about other people's behaviour, I'm simply the director of my own.

CONFESSION #449 ...

MY RELATIONSHIP VOWS

It is my joyful pleasure to give you the freedom to feel NO OBLIGATION whatsoever to support me, to provide for me, to love me, to cherish me, to be faithful to me or to make me happy. It's my responsibility to give those things to myself first and to allow you the space to give them as a precious gift in any moment that it feels good to freely express who you really are inside.

To me, a relationship is one where I give my mate more freedom to be whoever they choose to be in each given moment --- and still be accepted and loved anyway.

CONFESSION #450 …

I'VE SET YOU FREE

… to be yourself, to do what feels right for you, to decide what's important and to honour the calling of your own soul. I resonate with an expanded form of relationship where we feel secure enough give each other the freedom to stay or to go in any given moment, that this choice can never really be forced or commanded, that even if life were to change in an instant we both have the right to choose again that which is the most important path for us to take.

CONFESSION #451 ...

I MAKE THE MOST OF EVERY SITUATION

I acknowledge the downsides, but concentrate on the upsides.
Notice the disadvantages, but focus attention on the advantages.
Be aware of the problem, but talk so much more about the solution.
Accept the worst that can happen, but vividly imagine the best possible outcome.
Ask the question, and then be open to receiving the answer ... and it's always given in more appropriate ways than I had even wished for.

CONFESSION #452 ...

I EXPECT GOOD THINGS TO HAPPEN

... and as I move forward through my life I notice the evidence of profound blessings, attract more magnificent adventures, immerse myself in creative pastimes, feel deeper passion, bask in the fulfilment of intimately loving relationships, weave closer friendships, enjoy expanded financial freedom, create more positive outcomes, feel a stronger sense of purpose, revel in who I am and find so many extra reasons to laugh my head off ... lol

CONFESSION #453 ...

OH MY GOD, I'VE JUST REALISED SOMETHING IMPORTANT

Attracting something "bad" into my life is NOT an indication I've done something wrong, it's an indication that I've been reaching for something so incredible, that this is the quickest path to get there.

CONFESSION #454 ...

THERE'S NOTHING I NEED TO GO BACK AND FIX

… there's just something so much more inspiring, fulfilling and heart-warming to look forward to.

CONFESSION #455 ...

WHEN SOMEONE HAS HURT ME

1. Forgive them (for they know not what they do).
2. Be thoughtful to apologise for the times I've hurt others.
3. Remember to forgive myself for the mistakes I've made too.
4. Stay open.
5. Protect from further hurt by taking care of my own needs first.
6. Take as much time as I need to recover.
7. Look for the blessings as soon as I can.
8. Only take action when in an emotionally stable state.
9. Open my heart bigger than ever before.

CONFESSION #456 …

I DON'T CARE WHAT "YOU" DO

… I just care that what I'M doing feels right for me.

CONFESSION #??? ...

I'VE WRITTEN SO MANY CONFESSIONS

... sometimes I wonder what number I'm up to ... lol

CONFESSION #457 ...

WHAT OTHER PEOPLE ARE ATTRACTING IS THEIR OWN BUSINESS

… what I'm attracting is mine. It feels better to be thoughtful than to be blunt, it feels better to hope than to condemn, it feels better to praise than to criticize, it feels better to love than to hate. It feels so much better to let people live their own lives and for me to focus on living mine.

CONFESSION #458 ...

I'M PERFECT, JUST THE WAY I AM

There's nothing I need to change, nothing I need to do.
Life provides the ideal platform to keep recreating myself anew.
Each moment I can choose to direct my thoughts, to align,
to connect to universal intelligence and to access wisdom from the divine.

I think that being true to myself is the same as being whole,
when I'm doing what feels right for me, I connect more intimately to my soul.
Love always beckons me nearer, no matter how far off track I might go
and I appreciate life's contrast for giving me the greatest opportunities to grow.

CONFESSION #459 ...

THERE'S SOMETHING SO MUCH BETTER IN FRONT OF ME

… than anything I've left behind.

As I focus my attention forward, I can sense a soothing peace, greater joy, the softest bliss, a smoother path, enhanced understanding, harmonious communications, a sweetly aligned relationship, gentle growth, more fun, louder laughter, a happier home, grander ecstasy and greater love flowing in, around and through me more than ever before.

CONFESSION #460 ...

I LOVE THE AGE I AM

... an age where wisdom enhances my body and my mind, an age where beauty can be found more visibly on the inside and out, an age where each extra year means I've gained extra life experience and an age where getting older gives me the opportunity to add more value to this world than I'll ever know.

CONFESSION #461 ...

IN EACH MOMENT I HAVE TWO CHOICES

I can wait for something or someone to change before I feel better OR I can change my mind about what it all means and make myself feel better right now.

CONFESSION #462 ...

LAUGHTER AND SEX ARE THE BEST THERAPY

… to release resistant thoughts, to break constant patterns, to change rigid beliefs, to lighten the mood, to relax the pressure, to expand the energy, to strengthen the bond. When times get tough, I prefer to look for the light through the darkness, notice the humour in the seriousness, find the blessings in the turmoil and feel my way into a heavenly good orgasm – either self-inflicted or shared!

CONFESSION #463 …

I'M SO SURE OF WHO I AM

I DON'T TRY TO GET OTHER PEOPLE TO APPROVE OF ME … What they think of me is none of my business, BUT what I think about myself means everything.

I DON'T NEED TO GET OTHER PEOPLE TO AGREE WITH ME … I'm having fun finding my own integrity that I can allow them the space to discover theirs too.

I DON'T NEED OTHER PEOPLE TO LOVE ME … I love MYSELF so much, it makes them wonder what my secret is.

CONFESSION #464 ...

I HAVE A GOOD TIME WHEREVER I GO

I don't wait for other people to change, for my environment to be better, for my bank balance to increase, for my relationships to improve before I can have a good time. I decide to have a good time anyway, and then more good feeling things are attracted into my life to match exactly where my vibration is at.

CONFESSION #465 ...

MY GOAL

... is not to change the world, to reach enlightenment, to achieve perfection or even to teach what I know ... my goal in each moment is simply to feel a little better than I did the moment before. My greatest pleasure hasn't come from setting big goals or from reaching them; instead, it comes from appreciating as much as I can about each small step along the way.

CONFESSION #466 ...

LIFE JUST GOT SO MUCH BETTER

... when I stopped being so hard on myself and started to appreciate just how far I've really come.

CONFESSION #467 …

I ONLY HAVE ONE REASON TO DO ANYTHING

… because it feels good, because it brings me joy, because it seems "right", because it lights up my life, because it draws a smile, because it makes me laugh, because it delights my senses, because it turns me on, because it warms my heart, because it sets my spirit free.

CONFESSION #468 ...

I'VE FALLEN IN LOVE ALL OVER AGAIN

... with myself, with life, with being free, with living as if nothing really matters yet every moment is divinely precious.

I FOUND MY SOUL MATE

... who believes in me even more than I believe in myself, who is constantly close by to listen, to understand, to care, to comfort ... someone who I can trust with my deepest desires, who always wants the best for me, who loves me completely and will never leave me ...

... and was inside me all along!

(A soul mate comes along when we've released any resistance to receiving what the universe created for us the moment we wished for it. There's not only one perfect person out there, it's about being the perfect person ourselves, then the right one just shows up, no effort at all).

CONFESSION #469 …

I LOVE BEING IN LOVE

… to give love, be love, share love, make love … to weave the passion, to do what feels right, to plan for the future and to live for the moment, to find the peace, to feel the fullness, to laugh out loud, to cry in the stillness, to enjoy our reality and to indulge in fantasy, to fight in the fury, to make up in the rawness of ecstasy. I love it all … thank you!

CONFESSION #470 ...

I USED TO THINK I WAS WISE

.. that I should decide which things are good or bad, right or wrong, better or worse and then to plan my life accordingly. But real wisdom doesn't come from the mind in preparation of the future as a result of the past; real wisdom rises from the heart, it is born out of the newness of each precious moment and inspired intrinsically from the raw emotion of the present.

CONFESSION #471 ...

I DECIDE WHAT I WANT TO BELIEVE

... and then find all the evidence in the world to support it.

CONFESSION #472 ...

I'M A BLASPHEMER

I'm forever taking the lords name in vain, especially during moments of intense passion ... oh god, oh god, oh my god ... lol

CONFESSION #473 ...

THERE ARE TIMES WHEN I'VE WANTED SOMETHING SO MUCH

... that there was no room for doubt, no space for disappointment, no opportunity to lose hope, no need to talk about the past, no chance to go back ... just a gentle desire to allow myself to experience all the ins and outs associated with living, laughing, learning and loving in the most divinely delightful way.

CONFESSION #474 ...

I HAPPILY THREW MY MORALS OUT THE WINDOW

… and now use my gut instincts in each moment to determine if something feels right to me. I don't inflict my awareness on others or decide others are wrong for the choices they make, for in the very next moment, we each have the chance to choose again the way of being that works best for us.

Morals are created by "THINKING about the pain of the past" and take time to assess, analyse and rationalize. Gut instincts come from "FEELING the fullness of the present moment" and to know instinctually what to be, do, have or choose next.

CONFESSION #475 ...

I'M ALWAYS HOME

My physical body may move from one country to another, but my spiritual certainty of who I am, what I want and where I fit into this world, still remains the same.

CONFESSION #476 ...

I REGULARLY INDULGE

... in things that others would consider are "bad" for me and savour every delicious moment.

Feeling pleasure always has positive outcomes, but it's the "guilt" I create by focusing on the perceived negative effects afterwards that hurts. So I decided to STOP over-indulging in thoughts of guilt and START making peace with what I do instead!

CONFESSION #477 ...

I FEEL FABULOUS

... but then I always sleep when my mind tells me, eat what my body calls for and take time to reconnect when my spirit slips away from me.

WHEN I DON'T FEEL FABULOUS

... I don't write about it, talk about it, share it, find reasons for it, expand on it, I just take time out until I do feel better and then I make those good feelings larger than life.

CONFESSION #478 …

MY ONLY WISH FOR YOU is what you would wish for yourself, multiplied by all the stars in the sky.

CONFESSION #479 ...

I LOVE MY LIFE

Not because something special happened, not because I saw the sunrise this morning, not because I breathed more deeply, not because I stopped to smell the roses, not because I enjoyed great sex today, not even because I'm blessed ... but just because I CHOOSE to declare it often, declare it openly, declare it loudly and make it true.

CONFESSION #480 ...

WHEN I BELIEVE THAT LIFE IS ALWAYS WORKING OUT FOR ME

... answers are often given before the question has even been asked, solutions are presented before the problem has even been fully realized, messages are received without knowing who they're directly for and my day's been enhanced before it's even begun.

TRUSTING THAT SOMETHING GOOD WILL COME OUT OF THIS

... gives me a sense of relief, a moment to release my worries, let go my concern and open to an even better solution.

CONFESSION #481 ...

I'M AMAZING AND SO ARE YOU

Whenever I notice your negative traits, I put a spotlight on my own and push us further apart.

Whenever I highlight your positive aspects I expand my own, bring us closer together and make the world an even nicer place to be.

CONFESSION #482 ...

I DON'T NEED ANYTHING TO BE DIFFERENT

I don't need anything to be different ... I'm happy with life just the way it is!
I don't need anyone else to change ... Who they are being doesn't impact on who I know I am!
I don't need any situation to be better ... I accept it as part of my magnificent journey and appreciate fully each extra breath I get to breathe along the way!

CONFESSION #483 ...

I ALWAYS KNOW WHAT TO DO NEXT

... because it makes me "feel good" to think about it. I never take action until that moment arrives; then I know with certainty that I'm divinely guided, from the inside out.

CONFESSION #484 ...

I WAIT UNTIL IT FEELS RIGHT

Most of us were taught to take action, and then be happy about it ... I get happy about what I've already got first, and then the next action to take is so obvious, so intoxicating, so "right for me", I feel compelled to do it.

CONFESSION #485 ...

WHEN I WANT MY CIRCUMSTANCES TO BE DIFFERENT

... I start telling an uplifting new story; to gain a different perspective of what's happened in the past, to modify my perception of the present and to shine a light towards my dream for the most wonderful future imaginable.

CONFESSION #486 …

IT'S EASY TO HAVE MORE OF THE GOOD THINGS IN LIFE

I love having fun … let's do more of that.
I thrive on uplifting conversations … let's have more of those.
I get a buzz when I find solutions for my challenges … let's relax and allow more of them.
I adore feeling good … let's decide to be light-hearted, appreciate what we already have, enjoy the simple things in life and inspire others along the way.

CONFESSION #487 ...

I KNOW HOW TO HANDLE A CRISIS

I could run around trying to work out what's gone wrong, wonder why someone else is doing what they're doing, get a counsellor to try to analyse the issue, ask other people their opinion and further "activate" the problem ... OR I can relax a little, breathe deeper, speak less, look after myself more, take some time out and "allow" the solution to find me.

CONFESSION #488 …

I LOVE MY FREEDOM

to pretend that things are better than they seem,
to imagine I have everything I could possibly want,
to act as if my life is divine,
to play as if I don't have a worry in the world

oh, hang on, I've been pretending so long it's all come true!

CONFESSION #489 ...

I ACCEPT EVERYTHING AS IT IS RIGHT NOW

I don't wish for other people to be different; I focus my attention on the aspects I prefer and stimulate their better side instead.

I don't waste energy by remembering my past failures, I find more success in dreaming of a brighter future.

I don't keep talking about problems, I relax and allow the solutions to come through me.

I don't wait for situations to change before I can have a feeling of comfort in my heart, I find an abundance of peace as I look around for endless things to appreciate instead.

I don't expect other people to make me happy, I feel incredible as I consistently choose to experience happiness inside, no matter what is happening outside.

In doing this, I remember the magnificent creator I really am and set everyone else free to remember their magnificence too.

CONFESSION #490 ...

SOMETIMES I JUST HAVE TO STOP FOR A FEW MOMENTS

... and think about where I've come from, how many wonderful experiences I've had, how MUCH I've been given, the peace, harmony and love that exists in my life right now and the incredible gifts that are still on their way to me. There's always MORE to create, things always get easier, life always gets richer for me.

CONFESSION #491 ...

I NEVER NEED COURAGE

Courage is only required if I choose to take action BEFORE my thoughts, beliefs and attitudes are aligned with what I really want for my life. When I align my beliefs FIRST, courage is never needed as the action is inspired from inside, it stimulates my deepest passion and also seems like the next most obvious step.

CONFESSION #492 ...

MY TEN COMMANDMENTS (simple strategies to help me live a more fulfilled life)

1. Breathe deeper (always helpful unless I'm underwater).
2. Take notice of what I'm thinking and make sure it's about things I DO want, not about what I don't.
3. Only get involved in conversations that are uplifting.
4. Write down the positive aspects of every situation that's causing me discomfort.
5. Spend as much time as possible appreciating everything I've already been given and being thankful for what's still to come.
6. Make sure my beliefs line up with what I want for my life.
7. Allow other people the space to grow, to live their own lives and NOT become dependent on me for anything.
8. Give to myself first. When I fill myself up, the overflow naturally showers others.
9. Be authentic. Follow my bliss. Live the life that's right for me, in tune with my own integrity.
10. Do whatever it takes to align myself with my creator/ inner self/ God/ love and then allow all thoughts, words and actions be inspired from that place of deeper knowing.

CONFESSION #493 ...

I CELEBRATE EVERY DAY

I don't wait for a birthday to appreciate someone's life. I don't wait for an anniversary to value the positive aspects of my relationship. I don't wait for Christmas to give someone a surprise they really want and I don't wait for something good to happen before I feel like being happy! I'm happy just to be alive!

CONFESSION #494 ...

I HAVE A SELECTIVE MEMORY

… for the things that bring me joy, for the feelings that still my mind, for the words that brighten my day, for the beauty that makes me smile, for the peace that warms my soul and for the love that fills my heart … You know that disagreement we had yesterday? I can't even remember what it was about. My selective memory sorted that all out!

CONFESSION #495 ...

I KNOW THE DIFFERENCE BETWEEN AN EXCEPTIONAL RELATIONSHIP AND AN ORDINARY RELATIONSHIP

My attitude about it, the thoughts I choose to think about it, the conversations I allow myself to be involved in about it and the "knowing" that we each have the ability to enhance or detract from the quality of every interaction we're involved in.

CONFESSION #496 ...

I DON'T BELIEVE IN KARMA OR DESTINY

My world isn't guided by something I did in a previous life, something I once thought that has tainted my future, something I once said that will never be forgiven or something that someone else chose for me to experience instead. In each given moment I have the power to know whether I'm moving towards a destiny I want, or a destiny I don't want, simply by noticing how I'm feeling.

Choosing "thoughts", speaking "words" and doing "deeds" that bring relief, that make me feel better, that open my heart wider is the easiest way to consciously focus towards the destiny of my dreams, moment by blessed moment.

CONFESSION #497 ...

THERE'S SOMETHING SO MUCH BETTER WAITING FOR ME

… because I decided to believe it, I started to imagine it, I began to feel it, I focused my attention towards it, I made an effort to keep affirming it, I found many examples of it and I allowed it to become part of my new story ... then I came to know it and I made it happen … but it wasn't "out there somewhere" waiting for me, I found it "inside" first and the rest is history.

CONFESSION #498 ...

I DO WHATEVER FEELS RIGHT FOR ME IN THE MOMENT

... with no great plans, no preconceived notions, no pertinent goals, no hidden agendas, no expectations of others, just a deep sense of faith that I am more expertly guided through life by listening to the calling of my soul.

CONFESSION #499…

I LIVE LIFE ON MY TERMS … in a state of eternal freedom, never to allow the constraints, judgments or expectations of others, limit who I know myself to be.

I NEVER aim for less than what I truly desire.
I GIVE what I want, when I want, to whoever I want, as often as I want and I'm open to receive as well.
I tell the TRUTH to myself no matter how much I think it might hurt.
I search for the POSITIVE ASPECTS in everything.
I ACCEPT we are all doing the very best we can, no matter what crazy behaviours we sometimes demonstrate.
I WON'T pretend to be less than the incredible person I know I am just so someone else can feel better.
I ADORE myself, but if others don't, that's OK too.
I'm open to find HAPPINESS, ECSTASY and BLISS in as many places as I can.
I APPRECIATE everything I've already been given … even if I might not understand its' benefits at the time.
I'm THANKFUL for what I'm about to receive.
I choose to find something to LAUGH about every day.
I DO whatever it takes to be true to 'who I really am'.
I IMAGINE myself living the most enchanting life and allow the universe to orchestrate the finer details.
I can EXPERIENCE the darkest despair and then rise from the ashes and know my higher self is always shining a light for me.
I LOVE unconditionally, without expecting anything in return.
I find as many reasons as possible to PRAISE myself and others.
I intend to be an UPLIFTING influence in the lives of those I touch.

I look for the MAGNIFICENCE in nature and the BEAUTY in people all around me.
I KNOW my birthright is to be healthy and wealthy.
I FEEL my deepest passions and follow them with gentle persistence.
I LISTEN to the calling of my soul and surrender to it completely.

CONFESSION #500 ...

TODAY IS THE FIRST DAY OF A BRAND-NEW JOURNEY

... where I leave behind all unpleasant experiences from the past, pack and carry the memories I fondly cherish, make peace with what's happening in the present and decide which adventures I'll take in the future. No drama, no explanation, no more story to justify where I've come from, just a gentle moving towards something so much better.

To be continued ...

Note from the Author

Thank you so much for coming along and sharing your time with me. If you enjoyed a few laughs, discovered something new, received insights or found value from any of the Confessions in this book, don't keep it a secret, please take a moment to write a short review so others can find it too. It is greatly appreciated.

Elizabeth Richardson (ER)

https://elizabethrichardson.info
https://amazon.com/author/elizabethrichardson
https://youtube.com/user/elizabethrichardson
https://facebook.com/elizabeth.richardson.international
https://linkedin.com/in/elizabethrichardsonaustralia

www.ingramcontent.com/pod-product-compliance
Lightning Source LLC
Chambersburg PA
CBHW071654170426
43195CB00039B/2193